Introducti(

Barmouth (Abermaw) and the Mawdd rounding hills and mountains, is one of t Wales. Lying within the Snowdonia National Pa attracted many famous travellers and writers, with Wordsworth describing the estuary as 'sublime'. By the early 19thC Barmouth, then a thriving port with many shipyards operating along the estuary, was also emerging as a holiday resort as sea-bathing became fashionable. The arrival of the railway in 1867, crossing the magnificent railway viaduct, whilst precipitating the decline in the shipping industry, brought in many more visitors, drawn by sand, sea, the curative powers of scurvy grass, and the mountainous hinterland. Barmouth rapidly developed into an important Victorian sea-side resort.

Across the mouth of the estuary lies Fairbourne with its famous narrow gauge steam railway. Inland, the wooded slopes above the estuary rise north to the foothills of the Rhinogs, and south to the Cadair Idris range. These upland areas are crossed by important ancient trackways and are rich in prehistoric sites and monuments, including hillforts, standing stones and burial chambers. They also contain slate quarries, manganese workings and the famous gold-mines above Bontddu.

The 20 circular walks in this book comprehensively explore the area's wonderful combination of coast, estuary, hills, and upland valleys, and its fascinating history, using the network of good paths, ancient green upland roads, tramways and the former railway line, now the Mawddach Trail, running along the estuary. They offer superb views and pass many sites of historical interest. Most are accessible by public transport.

The routes, which range from a low-level 3-mile ramble to a 10-mile mountain circuit, follow public rights of way or permissive paths, and are within the capability of most people. *A key feature is individual routes, as well as containing shorter walk options, can easily be linked to provide longer and more challenging day walks.* Ensure you are suitably equipped and supplied, especially on the more exposed higher routes. Walking boots are recommended, along with appropriate clothing to protect against the elements. Please remember that the condition of paths can vary according to season and weather. If you encounter any problems with paths, please refer these to Gwynedd Council Highways Department (01341 422341).

Each walk has a detailed map and description which enables the route to be followed without difficulty, but be aware that changes in detail can occur at any time. The location of each walk is shown on the back cover and a summary of their key features is also given. This includes an estimated walking time, but allow extra time to enjoy the scenery. Please observe the country code.

DINAS OLEU & THE PANORAMA WALK

DESCRIPTION This 3¾ mile walk (**A**) features two of Barmouth's natural attractions, popular with visitors since the 19thC – Dinas Oleu, the rugged hillside overlooking the town and the first property given to the National Trust after its foundation in 1895; and the famous Panorama Walk – both offering stunning views of the area. Allow about 2¼ hours. A shorter 1¼ mile walk of Dinas Oleu (**B**) is included.
START Tourist Information Centre/Railway Station, Barmouth. [SH 613159]

Dinas Oleu was donated by Mrs Fanny Talbot and aptly fulfills the stated desire of creating 'open-air sitting rooms for city dwellers to have a place to breathe'. She also gave 13 cottages to her close friend, writer, art critic and social reformer John Ruskin to further his experiments in social living. One of his first tenants was Auguste Guyard, known locally as 'The Frenchman' He worked tirelessly, instructing local people on horticultural matters and the virtues of a frugal industrious life, until his death in 1883. He is buried on the hillside. Mothers used to bring children suffering from whooping cough onto Dinas Goleu to benefit from the seaborne air.

I Go along Station Road towards Barmouth's main street. At the junction, turn RIGHT, then take the first road on the left (Water Street). Shortly, turn LEFT up Tan-y-Graig and follow the oak leaf Dinas Oleu signs, soon leaving the tarmaced lane to go up a path. Shortly, the path swings sharp LEFT up to reach an information board at a good viewpoint. With your back to the information board go up the path past the metal NT Dinas Oleu sign. Shortly at a path junction keep ahead across the gorse covered

hillside, soon bending sharp RIGHT to angle up the hillside. You pass a side path on the left, then one on your right, before bending LEFT to reach a stone semi-circular viewing platform – *built in 1995 to commemorate the National Trust's centenary, it offers splendid views overlooking Barmouth, the mouth of the Mawddach estuary to Fairbourne and along the coast to Pembokeshire. Also northwards to Shell Island, and the Lleyn Peninsular extending to Bardsey Island. Near the harbour is the distinctive old Round House, built in 1834.* Return down the path and turn LEFT on the first side path. Follow it across the slope and down to go through a small gate in the wall.

2 Continue with the path past the entrance to the Frenchman's Grave – *which you may wish to visit.* Keep on with the path alongside the wall. Just after passing a seat - *a good place to stop to take in the views across the Mawddach estuary to the Cadair Idris range –* at a waymarked path junction, take the LEFT fork. (*For **Walk B** continue straight ahead and follow the path down. Just before a small metal gate, turn right to rejoin **Walk A** on a descent down the '100 steps'.*) Follow the path up to go through a small metal gate. Keep on with the path angling up the hillside. After about 50 yards, it bends LEFT up nearer the wall, before moving away to rise steadily across the attractive craggy gorse and heather covered hillside to go through a small metal gate in the wall. Continue up the path to go through another gate. Follow the path up beneath 'The Slabs' – *popular with rock climbers –* to reach a lane.

3 Turn RIGHT and follow the lane down the hillside to a junction with Panorama Road. Turn RIGHT down the road, past the SNP Panorama car park to turn LEFT down through a gate on the waymarked Panorama Walk. Follow the delightful green path up the hillside and on to enter a wood and down between walls to go through a large wooden gate. Immediately turn RIGHT through an adjoining metal gate – signposted Panorama Walk. *In the early 1880s, a penny was charged by Mr Davies of the Corsygedol Hotel for entry via a 'toll-wicket' here, causing*

2

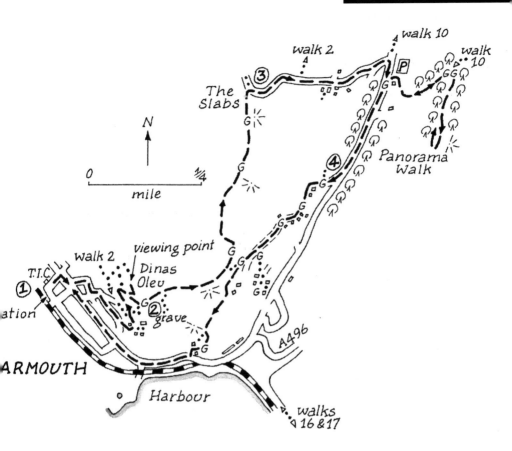

people to grumble and write to the papers. *A commentator at the time said that without his enterprise the 'View' would have been lost to the public altogether!* Follow the path up through the trees. When it splits, take the LEFT fork and follow a part-stepped path up past a seat up on to the open rocky summit, *where a wooden seat makes an excellent stopping place to take in the magnificent views over the tidal Mawddach estuary to the coast.* Complete the Panorama circuit of the hilltop, and retrace your steps back to the road. Continue down the road, past the entrance to Hafod-y-Bryn.

4 At a footpath post on the right, take the track angling up from the road. Just before a house, turn RIGHT up steps and through a metal gate. Follow the fence to pass behind the house. At the fence corner, turn LEFT down between walls and through a large wooden gate. Continue ahead past a house, and at another house just ahead, bear RIGHT along a stony track, through a gate, and on up the track. Follow the track down to a private gateway. Here, turn RIGHT to go through a small metal gate. Turn LEFT (or continue ahead to return along your outward route). Walk alongside the wall, through a small metal gate, past a house, and on down to reach an open aspect by a disused quarry - with good views over the harbour. Take the waymarked LEFT fork of the path to soon go down the stepped path, known locally as the '100 Steps' to the main road. Follow it RIGHT back into the centre of Barmouth.

3

CERRIG ARTHUR & BWLCH-Y-LLAN

DESCRIPTION A 6 mile walk (**A**) exploring the fascinating attractive foothills above Barmouth offering stunning panoramic views. This meandering route easily divides into shorter described walks of 2¼ miles (**B**) and 4¼ miles (**C**). The route climbs up the rugged hillside of Dinas Oleu and on up to 'The Slabs', popular with rock climbers. It then continues up across upland pasture before descending to follow a scenic high-level road to its end, and on to Cerrig Arthur stone circle. The return route rises steadily on an ancient way to Llanaber church across open slopes to its highest point at 1115 feet, then descends Bwlch-y-Llan, before meandering on superb green tracks and paths back to Barmouth, taking in a small side peak on route. Allow about 4 hours for the main walk.

START Tourist Information Centre/Station, Barmouth [SH 613159]

Cerrig Arthur, set high on the open hillside, is the remains of a Bronze Age circle, possibly a ritual or burial monument. It also lies on the ancient upland route via Bwlch y Llan (the Pass to the Church) followed by inhabitants of Bontddu – a distance of over 5 miles – to worship in the 13thC parish church at Llanaber. Interestingly, the stones stand near the original site planned for Llanaber church, and are known as 'Church Stones'. According to tradition, its foundations were repeatedly demolished at night by an unseen power. The subsequent hearing of a voice crying 'Llanaber, Llanaber' made the terrified men change the location for their parish church.

I Follow the detailed instructions of paragraphs **I** and **2** in **Walk A** to reach the lane by 'The Slabs'. (*For Walk B, turn left – soon passing a ladder-stile on your left, offering an alternative link path, wet in plac-*

*es] – and follow the lane/track to Gellfawr farm. Just after passing in front of the house, turn left between a wall and an outbuilding, to rejoin the main route at point **5**.*)

2 For **Walk A** turn RIGHT down the lane, cross a stile by a gate, and on with the lane. Soon, go through a small metal gate on the left by a footpath post. Follow the waymarked path up the hillside to reach a superb viewpoint. The delightful path then rises along a small ridge, before levelling out to go through a gap in the wall. *Ahead is the distant ridge leading up to Diffwys.* After going through another wall gap, the path bends LEFT alongside the wall to cross a ladder-stile. Keep ahead to reach a wall corner beneath a transmitter mast. (*For Walk C, turn left alongside the wall. At its corner, follow a green path up the hillside ahead to go through a kissing gate in a wall. Rejoin the main route just ahead. Turn left and resume text at point **4**.*)

3 For **Walk A**, cross the ladder-stile and follow the path between walls. It soon bears LEFT and descends the hillside to a road. Follow the road ahead, past cottages, and on up to its end by Sylfaen farm. Here, take the waymarked path on the left along a stony track. After going through a gate, go half-LEFT off the track to follow a green track up to Cerrig Arthur. Just before the stones, turn LEFT through a large wooden gate. Follow the wall on your left and on past a ruined barn. Keep on with a track – *the old church route* – across the high upland pasture. After going through a gate by sheepfolds, continue ahead on a clear path up the hillside – *enjoying extensive views* – and on over two ladder-stiles. The path now levels out and goes along a small ridge, passing a kissing gate in the wall on your left.

4 Continue ahead, soon bearing RIGHT near the wall corner. The delightful path now descends Bwlch-y-Llan. After a while, turn sharp LEFT down a path to cross a ladder-stile by a gate. Continue on a delightful green path, soon descending to cross a ladder-stile, and on with a green track down to Gellfawr farm. Pass between an outbuilding and the end of the house, then turn RIGHT on the waymarked path.

5 Go past another outbuilding, and at a waymarked fence corner, turn LEFT alongside the fence down to go through a small metal gate and over a tiny stone bridge. Go through a rushy area to bear RIGHT through a gate in the wall, and follow a green track above a small wooded dingle. Just before a gap in a low wall, turn LEFT and follow the wall down to the ruins of Cellfechan farm. *In the 1920s the farm was owned by the Urban District Council and provided refreshments to passing walkers.* Just before the large stone barn on the seaward side, turn RIGHT through a wall gap. Go across

the field, through another wall gap and on to go through a small metal gate in the large wall ahead. Take the LEFT fork of the path

to reach a cairn on the top of Craig-y-Gigfran (Raven's Rock). *Known locally as 'The Peak', it offers superb views along the coast from the Lleyn Peninsular to Pembrokeshire. On the cairn is a plaque erected to the memory of soldiers from Birmingham killed in 1916.* Return to the barn.

6 Continue down the walled green track and through a gate. Follow this superb green track as it work its way down the hillside overlooking Barmouth, passing old manganese mine workings, to go through a small wooden gate, and on down a path to a lane. (*To maintain height a little longer, when the track bends sharp right, go up another green track, through a gate, and on with the track. Shortly go through a small gate in the wall below to reach the viewing platform again. Now follow a path right, soon descending via a zig-zag, to rejoin your main route by a metal fence. Follow it left to the lane.*) Turn RIGHT down the lane back to the start.

WALK 3
BWYLCH Y RHIWGYR

DESCRIPTION A 6½ mile walk exploring the foothills and high mountain passes north of Barmouth following ancient trackways, old bridleways, miners paths and tramways. It features an ancient hillfort and stone circle, extensive remnants of 19thC manganese mining, a 13thC church, and excellent views. The route rises to pass through Bwylch y Llan (1115 feet) before descending to Cerrig Arthur stone circle, part of an ancient route between Bontddu and the parish church at Llanaber. It then climbs up to the top of Bwylch y Rhiwgyr (1476 feet) before descending the narrow pass, used by drovers and travellers for centuries. It crosses high upland pasture, past substantial old manganese mine workings, before descending to Llanaber church, or on an alternative route. Allow about 4 hours. For experienced walkers.

START Lay-by, Llanaber [SH 605173]

DIRECTIONS Leave Barmouth on the A496 towards Harlech. Shortly after entering Llanaber, there is a lay-by on the left by a telephone box. Park tidily on the right side. The walk is also accessible by bus and train.

1 Cross the road and go up the access lane to Ceilwort Uchaf. Shortly, at a footpath post, go through a small metal gate, and follow a path alongside a stream, and on through a small gate above a garage. Now, bear RIGHT up the field edge, through a gateway, and on over a stream. Follow the wall up to cross a ladder-stile. Continue up the path, soon alongside a wall, to cross a ladder-stile. Keep ahead between two walls and on with the path to cross a ladder-stile. Turn RIGHT and follow a walled path up the hillside to meet a green track. Turn RIGHT along another walled track – *the church route* – to go through a gate.

2 Cross a nearby ladder-stile, and follow the old green trackway to rise steadily up the rocky hillside, later passing close to

a Romano British hillfort. You cross streams near an old incline, before bearing RIGHT to cross a ladder-stile. *Ore from the Hafotty manganese mine was brought down this gravity incline and continued on a tramway for a final descent by ropeway.* The track then crosses the hillside and passes a waymarked path junction to go up Bwylch y Llan. At the top of the pass follow the path round and on across a small ridge to cross a ladder-stile in the wall corner. Continue ahead – *with views over the Mawddach Estuary to Cadair Idris* – soon descending the hillside, to cross a ladder-stile and go through a gate by sheepfolds. Keep ahead alongside the wall, passing above a ruined stone barn and on to go through a gate in the wall corner to reach Carreg Arthur stone circle (see **Walk 2**).

3 Now turn LEFT up the slope to go through a gate. Continue up a green track to join a wall on your left. Shortly, go through a wooden gate in the wall by a post. Turn RIGHT and follow a path just above the wall. When it splits, take the LEFT fork and after about 20 yards, leave the path to angle slightly away from the wall over rough ground to cross two streams and then a stile in an old gateway. Go through wall gap ahead, then go half-LEFT up the tussocky slope and through a gate. Follow the green track up to go through a metal gate at the top of Bwylch y Rhiwgyr. Follow the path down the narrow pass.

4 After going through a metal gate, turn LEFT on a waymarked path. Keep close to the wall to cross a stone stile near the corner. Turn RIGHT, go through a wall gap, and keep ahead to join another path by a small pile of stones after about 75 yards. Follow this clear path across the slope, soon bending half-LEFT to drop down to a wall corner by

6

Walks 9 & 5

Walks 4 & 5

④ Bwlchy Rhiwgyr

·· walk 9

old workings

N

0   ¼
mile

old workings

ruin

⑤

Cerrig
⑥③ Arthur

walk 2

ruin

fort

Bwlch-
y-llan

incline

walk
2

underground and large opencast workings of the Hafotty mine (1885-94). It was the largest manganese mine in Merioneth, employing at its peak 37 men underground and 15 on the surface, producing 12,000 tons of ore for Mostyn Ironworks in Flintshire. Continue up the hillside to cross a ladder-stile.

5 Go half-LEFT across old workings, then keep with the RIGHT fork to descend the stony hillside to cross a ladder-stile. Go half-LEFT to follow a path initially towards a small stone enclosure, and on down through gorse to cross a ladder-stile. Continue ahead down a green track. When it bends right through a wet area, keep ahead through the reeds, then after about 20 yards, bear RIGHT, soon on a path through gorse to cross a ladder-stile. Now go half-RIGHT to follow a green track winding down the hillside. After it bends right, follow a choice of paths down through the gorse to go through a small metal gate in the field corner. Keep ahead, soon turning RIGHT through a gateway back on your outward route. Go along the walled track and on with the open track down upland pasture.

6 Just before a ladder stile by a gate, you have a choice. (For a more direct return turn left and drop down the hillside, soon joining a green track angling down to reach a familiar ladder-stile. Go through a small gate just below. Follow the path down the long narrow field, soon bearing right down to go through a small metal gate. Go down a narrow walled path, then track, passing behind Jesuits House to reach the A496. Turn left back to the start.) For Llanaber church – soon visible below – cross the ladder-stile and follow the track down the hillside. When it bends left, follow the waymarked path ahead to cross a ladder-stile. Keep ahead, then swing LEFT to go down a delightful walled bridleway. At the bottom bend RIGHT towards buildings. Turn LEFT through a gate and down a lane to cross the A496. Turn LEFT. After visiting the church continue along the road back to the start.

the remains of old workings. Here, go LEFT away from the wall corner past more workings, then follow the wall on your right. The Egryn manganese mine worked this area, mainly underground by levels and shafts in 2 periods: 1835-40 and 1917-24. From its northern end a 1¼ mile aerial ropeway took ore down to Egryn Abbey. Go ahead over 3 ladder-stiles to the top of the rise ahead. Now turn LEFT alongside the wall, and after 75 yards, bear half-RIGHT up the stone covered slope to join a level green track – a former 2ft gauge tramway. Turn RIGHT along the track passing close to old workings and on over a ladder-stile. Go half-LEFT with the old tramway and on down past a small ruin to cross a footbridge and ladder-stile beneath a heavily scarred slope. The area ahead contains deep

WALK 4

MYNYDD
EGRYN

DESCRIPTION A 4 mile walk on the foothills and upland shelf adjoining the coast between Llanaber and Tal-y Bont, featuring sites and monuments of significant archaelogical interest. The route passes the old house of Egryn Abbey, then rises steadily up to cross the expansive wild treeless exposed Mynydd Egryn, passing close to important prehistoric burial chambers to reach a Bronze Age ring cairn at a height of just over 1000 feet. The route then returns via the Iron Age fort of Pen y Dinas. Allow about 3 hours.

START Capel Egryn [SH 594205]

DIRECTIONS Take the A496 from Barmouth towards Harlech. Go through Llanaber and on past The Wayside, and the entrance to Trawsdir caravan/camping site. Shortly you will find a small lay-by on the right by an old chapel. The start is on a bus route – the stop is called 'Sunday School'.

I Cross the road and walk along the pavement back towards Barmouth. Shortly, turn LEFT along a track by a footpath post. Follow the track past the complex of buildings at Egryn Abbey, dating from the 16thC. *This site is reputed to have been an earlier grange of the Cistercian Cymmer Abbey and once a hospital for the poor and wayfarers.* When the main track bends left towards outbuildings, continue straight ahead on a stony track to go through a gate. Follow the track, bending RIGHT to cross over the Ceunant Egryn. Follow the track through another gate, past a large stone barn, and on alongside the river. Shortly, continue on the left of two green tracks rising up the hillside, past a telegraph pole. As the track bends up towards a gate, keep straight ahead to cross a stile in the wall, and on up to join a green track. Keep ahead. The track soon bends right and rises up the hillside, briefly running alongside a wall, before suddenly levelling out to give extensive all round views. *Ahead over the expanse of Mynydd Egryn is the long bare*

ridge leading up to Diffwys, and further north the rounded hill of Moelfre. There are views along the coast to Shell Island, the Lleyn peninsula, Bardsey Isand, and to the central mountains of Snowdonia. The slopes of the nearby Ceunant Egryn valley were worked for slate in the 1890s, employing 9 men, and later for manganese. Continue ahead on the faint green track.

2 When opposite the second of two stone circles on your right, bear LEFT over a drainage gully and keep on with a path. *Ahead on the skyline is the distinctive shape of Pen y Dinas prehistoric hillfort.* Shortly, bend RIGHT to go through a waymarked gate. Continue ahead on a path, over a waymarked footbridge, and on with a faint green track to reach a waymark post ahead. Cross a footbridge over another stream, and work your way across the reedy/tussocky terrain, wet in places, towards a distant metal inverted V pole. *Built of bullhead rails, this is the only remaining pylon – the rest were wooden – of the 1¼ mile aerial ropeway that carried ore down from the Egryn manganese mine to Egryn Abbey, from where it was taken by cart to Tal-y-Bont.* About 40 yards from the long wall, conditions underfoot improve and you can follow a clear path which takes you to the wall corner. *A little way to your left along the wall are the impressive Carneddau Hengwn burial chambers of multi-period construction, dating from the 3rd millennium.* From the wall corner, continue ahead on a clear path towards the distant ridge, soon going up a small stone and gorse covered rise to reach a Bronze Age ring cairn with its distinctive outward leaning stones. *It was used for burial and ceremonial purposes. Just to its east are the remains of a settlement enclosure.* Continue towards a ladder-stile by a gateway ahead, then turn LEFT alongside the wall to cross another ladder-stile in the wall corner. Keep ahead then swing LEFT away from another ladder-stile to follow a path for about 150 yards, dropping down a small stone encrusted slope.

3 Ignore the path going ahead parallel with the wall. Instead, head half-RIGHT across tussocky ground by the edge of an area

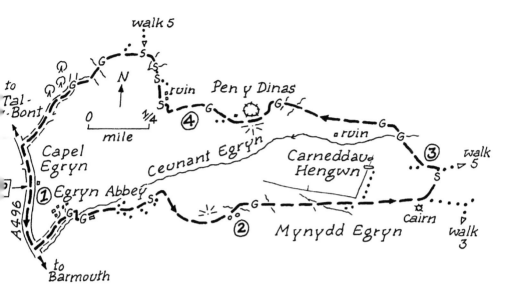

of gorse, and on to go through an old wooden gate in the wall by a small wet reedy area, and across the infant Ceunant Egryn. Go ahead for about 20 yards, then bear LEFT to follow a path through a gateway, and continue ahead on a green track – *with Carneddau Hengwn burial chambers visible to your left on the other side of the valley.* The green track runs between 50–75 yards from the wall on your right through the large field, before moving nearer the wall to fade in rushes by a stream. Continue near the wall, over another stream and on to cross a gate in the field corner. Turn LEFT past stone sheepfolds and on with a faint track through an old gateway. Keep ahead on the track to pass close to the southern slopes of Pen y Dinas hillfort to reach a prominent viewpoint. The green track now begins to descend, passing through the remains of an old wall. Just after passing a small ruin on your right, when the path bears half-left, keep straight on down towards a wall corner and on through a

small metal gate below. Go ahead down the hillside, passing close to a wall corner.

4 Keep on down the slope, moving slightly closer towards a ruined farmstead to drop down a track through gorse to reach a gap in an old wall, in line with the ruin. Turn RIGHT to cross a nearby ladder-stile. Go past the delightful ruin, and through an open gateway directly ahead, and on to cross a ladder-stile. Go along a track and over another ladder-stile by a stream. Continue with the track, over another stream, then shortly, cross a ladder-stile on the left. Follow this old walled bridleway down the hillside. Keep on with the wall on your left to go through a gate. Continue ahead on a faint green track, over a stream, and through an old gateway. Keep on down the next field to pass through gorse near a wall, and on through a metal gate onto a track. Follow it LEFT, and at a track junction bear RIGHT. Follow the track to the A496 and on along the pavement back to the start.

9

PEN Y DINAS

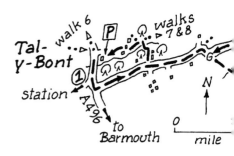

DESCRIPTION A 5¼ mile walk in the foot-hills adjoining the coast near Tal-y-Bont, featuring several ancient sites of archaelogical interest, and good views. The route heads inland up to the prehistoric hillfort of Pen y Dinas situated at over 750 feet. It then crosses a large expanse of more exposed upland pasture to visit a Bronze Age burial and settlement site, rising easily to a height of over 1200 feet to reach the ancient mountain trackway below Bwlch y Rhiwgyr. It returns by paths, tracks and lane past other ancient sites for a riverside finish. Allow about 4 hours.

START Tal-y-Bont [SH 589218]

DIRECTIONS From Barmouth take the A496 north towards Harlech. On entering Tal-y-Bont, just after passing over the river, there is a car park and toilets on the right.

1 Turn LEFT across the footbridge over the Afon Ysgethin and walk along the pavement by the A496. Shortly, turn LEFT along Ffordd Ty'n Fellin. Follow this country road for nearly ½ mile to pass the entrance to Ty'n Fellin. On the next bend, by a sign 'Hwylfa Porth Egryn' go through a wooden gate. Now follow a green track rising steadily up the hillside, through a gate and on up to go through another gate into a walled track. Turn RIGHT and follow the delightful green track across the hillside and over two ladder-stiles. As the track bends left up towards farm buildings, keep straight ahead to go through an old gateway. Continue past the ivy covered ruined upland farmstead and over a ladder-stile. Go half-LEFT a few yards, then bear RIGHT alongside the old wall.

2 After 15 yards, turn LEFT up a green track. When it fades, continue up the steep hillside, passing just to the right of a wall corner to go through a small metal gate. Continue ahead up the less steep slope on a faint path – *with the distinctive shape of Pen y Dinas ahead* – to join a faint green track, just to the right of a small low ruin. Follow it up to pass over the shoulder of the hill

– *with views ahead over Cwm Egryn to the long ridge leading up to Diffwys* – and on across the southern slopes of Pen y Dinas. *Strategically placed, this prehistoric hillfort has ramparts of earth and stone, with an entrance on its west side.* Keep with the green track near an old wall on your left to go through a gap in the wall ahead. Go on round the end of stone sheepfolds to go through a metal gate. Follow the wall on your left through the reed covered pasture. After crossing a second stream, follow an old green track, soon running between 75–50 yards from the wall. Later it moves back towards the wall to go through an old gateway. *On route, if you look half-right you can see the prehistoric burial chambers of Carneddau Hengwn on the other side of the valley.*

3 Keep ahead with the track for about 75 yards, then go half-RIGHT to cross the infant Ceunant Egryn and go through the old gate in the wall. Head half-LEFT across the tussocky terrain. Near to the far wall bear LEFT up the stone encrusted upland pasture parallel with the wall to a ladder-stile ahead. Before crossing this stile, turn RIGHT over a nearby stile into the adjoining field and on by the wall to visit a Bronze Age ring cairn with its distinctive outward leaning stones. *It was used for burial and ceremonial purposes. Just to its east are the remains of a settlement enclosure.* Retrace your steps, cross the first ladder-stile and go through a small gate on your left. Now go half-RIGHT, soon on a clear path. When it splits, keep on the RIGHT fork to cross an area of old manganese workings, and on with the path across the stone covered hillside, later rising closer to the wall up to your right to go through a small

half-LEFT for about 100 yards then go down the middle of a grassy ridge. At the bottom, swing RIGHT along a track to go through a gate.

5 Bear half-LEFT to follow a green track down to go through a wall gap. Continue

gate near the wall corner. Continue ahead to join the distinct path rising up Bwlch y Rhiwgyr by a waymark post. *This is an ancient mountain route connecting Harlech and the coast with Dolgellau* (see **Walk 9** for details).

4 Turn LEFT and follow the path down to go through a gate. The path continues alongside the wall, then becomes a green track, gently descending alongside a fence. At the end of the fence, leave the track and cross a ladder-stile into a field to follow the wall on your right. *The adjoining field contains the remains of two prehistoric religious and funerary stone circles.* The second half of the field is reedy, tussocky and wet in places. Cross a ladder-stile in the field corner, then go along the left bank of a stream to cross a ladder-stile and footbridge. Continue ahead to join a green track by the low mound of an old burial cairn. Continue down the track, and after about 50 yards, bear RIGHT on a path through the bracken. Drop down to cross a footbridge and on to go through a gate in the field corner (not the open gateway). Go

down the track, over an old boundary and through another wall gap. It then becomes a more distinct stonier track as it passes a ruin and descends the hillside. After passing through a gate, follow the track down to a farm. Turn RIGHT along its access track and on down the road, soon bending left and descending the hillside. *Shortly, to your left, in the trees, is the wall-topped circular embankment of an ancient farmstead.* Continue down the road, soon on your outward route. At a footpath post just before Annedd Wen, turn RIGHT through a small gateway and follow the narrow path to go across a footbridge over the river. Turn LEFT and follow the path alongside the river, through a gate, past another footbridge, and on between the beer garden and a small stone building to reach the Ysgethin Inn – *a former late 19thC woollen mill* – and the Country Museum (both worth a visit) before following the riverside path back to the start.

DYFFRYN BURIAL CHAMBERS

DESCRIPTION An easy 3 mile walk exploring the attractive countryside between Tal-y-Bont and Dyffryn Ardudwy, featuring impressive ancient burial chambers. Allow about 2 hours.

START Tal-y-bont [SH 589218] or Dyffryn Ardudwy [SH 587232]

DIRECTIONS From Barmouth take the A496 north towards Harlech. On entering Tal-y-Bont, just after passing over the river, there is a car park and toilets on the right.

At Dyffryn Ardudwy is an impressive rectangular Neolithic burial site dating from 4th /early 3rd millennium, but of multi-period construction. It contains two classic chamber tombs of the type (portal dolmens) most commonly found in this area, and on the east coast of Ireland, indicating a movement of early man across the Irish sea. Among the earliest tombs built in Britain, the lower of the Dyffryn tombs is the older, whilst the other has produced evidence of a late Bronze Age cremation. As man turned his activities from hunting to farming, and cleared woodland for pasture, settlements were established, and such tombs used for family burials over centuries became a focus for the local community, similar to the later role of churches. They feature tall entrance stones and a small rectangular chamber, generally covered by a large capstone, and are fine examples of early engineering. Such tombs were originally covered by a mound of stones or earth, but as a result of robbers, the chambers have been left exposed.

I Turn RIGHT along the A496 past the Post Office, then at the 40 mph road sign, turn RIGHT on a waymarked bridleway up a lane leading to Bellaport Caravan site. Follow this attractive tree-lined lane, and just beyond the last of a row of bungalows, cross a stone stile in the wall on your left. Go half-

RIGHT to go through a small metal gate in the wall. Go over an unusually broad section of stone wall into a field – *with good views to Shell Island and the Lleyn Peninsula beyond.* Continue ahead to go over a gated stile in another wide section of wall, and down steps into a field. Follow the wall on your right to go through a gate beneath a house, then go half-RIGHT up to join its access track. Follow it past farm buildings to a road and go through the gate.

2 Now bear RIGHT up the field to a waymark post by the top wall, about 50 yards from the field corner. Turn LEFT and walk alongside the wall, over the remains of another wall, and on with the waymarked path along the edge of a wood. Cross a stone stile into the wood and follow a path ahead through the trees. At a wall corner go half-LEFT across the field to pass through gorse to reach a small metal gate just ahead by the burial chambers. *From here you can see the jets manoeuvering at the airfield by Shell Island.* After visiting the site, follow the path down to the A496 at Dyffryn Ardudwy. Turn RIGHT along the road.

3 Take the first road on the left opposite a garage. Follow the road past cottages and a small crossroad out of the village. Then turn LEFT on a waymarked path at the end of a stone barn. Go over a stile and follow the boundary on your right past a gateway round to cross a gated stile. Turn LEFT along an access track, then bear RIGHT to a footpath post, and follow a path through the trees. Soon it bends RIGHT then LEFT to leave the wood by a small gate just before the railway line. Heed the warning signs to cross over the line. Now follow the path through the wood opposite, and on across a field to reach a road by Ty Bennar. Turn RIGHT along the road, and shortly, at the entrance to Bennar Fawr, go through an adjoining gate by a footpath sign. Go up the field to cross a stile in the wall ahead. Keep ahead alongside the wall and after about 50 yards, go half-RIGHT towards a telegraph pole to cross a stile in the wall. Walk through the field towards a house to cross a stone stile in the wall corner. Now turn LEFT along the edge of the large

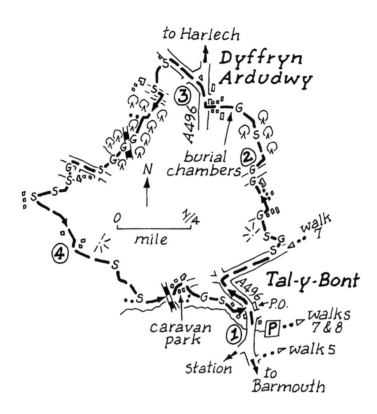

to Harlech

Dyffryn
Ardudwy

③ A496 G

burial ②
N chambers G

0   ¼
mile

④

walk 7

Tal-y-Bont
P.O.
caravan
park ①   P   walks 7 & 8

Station   to   walk 5
Barmouth

field and at a ditch go half-RIGHT to pass to the left of an isolated stone barn to reach a collection of farm buildings ahead.

4 Here go RIGHT and at the end of the barn, turn LEFT and walk ahead to a waymarked end of wall containing an old stone stile. *To the east is the rounded shape of Moelfre and ahead the long ridge leading up to Diffwys.* Now go almost half-LEFT across the field to go through a gated stile in the wall. Go half-RIGHT to a wall corner supporting a fence. Here, head half-LEFT to go through an old gateway in the wall corner, then bear RIGHT along the edge of the next field to cross a stone stile in the wall corner and on to a track. Follow it LEFT, soon

by the river, to pass under the railway line – *don't worry, it's higher than it looks!* – to reach Pandy caravan park. Turn LEFT along the lane, passing between farm buildings. With the camping office on your left, turn RIGHT through the static caravan park, keeping with the LEFT fork to go through a gate into a field, which is used for tourers and tents. Go up the field to cross a stile in the fence just before the top right hand corner by the river. Pass to the left of wooden chalets, and on past the old corn mill with its waterwheel, then Mill Cottage and up its access track to the road opposite the post office at Tal-y-bont.

13

WALK 7

COED
CORS-Y-GEDOL

DESCRIPTION A delightful 4¼ mile walk (**A**) or 3 mile walk (**B**) through broadleaf woodland and open country, passing Cors-y-Gedol, one of the area's most historic houses. The route takes you up through the wooded Afon Ysgethin valley to an old drovers halt, then passes a Neolithic burial chamber to reach Cors-y-Gedol. The main route explores the surrounding attractive countryside, before passing through further woodland on its return. Allow about 2½ hours. The route also includes an alternative 2½ mile woodland circuit (**C**).
START Talybont [SH 589218]
DIRECTIONS See **Walk 6**.

For centuries Cors y Gedol was home to the Vaughans, one of the principal families of Ardudwy. They were descendants of Osborn Fitzgerald (Wyddel), an Irish nobleman, who came to Wales in the 13thC, and who acquired the estate through marriage. Centuries ago most of the surrounding land was marshy, which could help to explain its name meaning 'The bog of hospitality'. For many years they played a prominent role in Meirioneth affairs, serving as MPs, High Sheriffs and Magistrates. In 1791 the family died out and the estate passed to the Mostyns, another aristocratic family, who lived here until 1860. The current mansion, dating from 1576, has undergone considerable alteration and extension, with additional houses and agricultural buildings, reflecting the acquired wealth of successive generations. It lies at the end of a straight drive connecting it with the Vaughan family chapel in Llanddwywe church.

I From the end of the car park, turn LEFT on a path beside the Afon Ysgethin to reach a large car park. Continue ahead, passing close to the Ysgethin Inn – *a former late 19thC woollen mill, whose porch was built with stone taken from an old drover's inn, Rhos-caerau, on the upland route to*

Bontddu. Pass the entrance to the Rural Life Museum and go round the right hand end of a small stone building just ahead to rejoin the river. Follow the main path through the attractive wood, with the river never very far away. Go over a ladder-stile and on with the path. After a while, the path rises away from the river to reach a path junction by a seat. Continue ahead on the wide level path, with the river rising steadily to join you once more. Keep with the main path close by the river, rising to another path junction. (*For* **Walk C** *turn left up the path and follow it back along the top edge of the wood. Shortly, take the left fork of the path on a gentle descent. At a distinct cross-path, turn right and follow a narrow path through the trees, over a faint cross path. At another path junction keep ahead, and after a further 100 yards, you rejoin the main route just before a stream and a gate. Here swing sharp left and resume text at the 3rd sentence in paragraph 4.*) For the main route, continue ahead above the river, through a wooden gate, and on up to reach a lane by Lleti Lloegr – *The English Shelter* – which was once an an emergency shoeing station and overnight stopping place for 17th/18thC drovers heading for the mountain pass of Bwlch y Rhiwgyr on route to Bontddu. Cattle were kept in five adjoining small fields.

2 Turn LEFT along the lane, past a Neolithic burial chamber, dating from 4th/3rd millennium BC, and on through a gate to a road. *Here are extensive views of the vast upland landscape, with the rounded hilltop of Moelfre, and, further inland, the long ridge leading to Diffwys and the distant mountains of Snowdonia ahead.* Turn LEFT down the road to the first bend by an entrance to Cors y Gedol. Here you have a choice. (*For* **Walk B**, *continue on the road, passing numerous stone buildings, then Llys Faen to reach an ornate stone gateway by a track to Meifod Uchaf. Continue along the straight section of road. After about 200 yards, turn left through a gate by a footpath post to rejoin* **Walk A** *at point 4.*) For **Walk A**, go straight ahead on a waymarked path along the track to the buildings of Cors y Gedol. Bend RIGHT with the track past a

reach a road. Turn LEFT and follow this quiet country road past Meifod Isa farm. Just before a gate on the lane, take the waymarked bridleway through a gate on the left. Go half-RIGHT across the field, then shortly, go towards the left-hand end of the boundary wall of a small wood ahead, and follow this delightful bridleway through the attractive part wooded terrain. After crossing a stile, continue ahead alongside a fence and on through a gate onto a road by Parc Uchaf. Turn LEFT along the leafy road. Shortly, take a waymarked path through a gate on the right into the wood.

4 Keep ahead on a clear path to go through a gate and over the stream. Now bear RIGHT on a wide stony path alongside the stream. Follow this path through the wood. At a crossroad of paths, take the RIGHT fork, cross a footbridge over the stream, and on through a small gate at the edge of the wood by Bellaport caravan site. Go ahead down an attractive straight walled lane – *enjoying your last views along the coast and across Cardigan Bay* – to reach the A496. Turn LEFT and walk along the pavement the short distance back to the start.

house and keep ahead to go through a metal gate. Follow the boundary wall on your left, through a gate, and on with boundary to cross a stone stile in the field corner. Go half-RIGHT to join a cross-path by a stream in an area of gorse. Turn LEFT and follow this stony path through the gorse – *with good views of Shell Island, the Lleyn Peninsula and Bardsey Island* – to go through a gate in a wall corner. Continue alongside the wall on your left.

3 At the wall corner, bear RIGHT, soon passing between a short section of old boundaries, then follow the old wall on your left. At its corner, keep straight ahead to

15

WALK 8
CWM YSGETHIN

DESCRIPTION This route offers a choice of two great upland walks from Cwm Ysgethin: a 7 mile walk (**A**) featuring the ancient stone bridge of Pont Scethin set in splendid isolation at 1036 feet, and an energetic 9 mile walk (**B**) taking in the Llawlech ridge (1932 feet) running between two historic mountain passes. The shared outward route follows the course of the Afon Ysgethin, initially through attractive woodland, then follows an old drovers route across the wild expansive bare upland valley past Llyn Erddyn, set amidst the foothills of the Rhinogs, to meet the ancient Harlech-Dolgellau-London road. Walk A then crosses over Pont Scethin, follows a section of the old road, before gently descending an upland bridleway and passing historic Cors Y Gedol for a woodland finish. Walk B follows the old road up past the Janet Haigh memorial to the bwlch, then crosses the ridge to descend to Bwlch y Rhiwgyr. From here it returns down another ancient route, then paths and lane. Allow about 4 hours (**A**) and 6 hours (**B**). See **Walk 9** for information on the ancient roads, and use its map for **Walk B**. These routes are easy to follow but should be avoided in poor visibility. For experienced walkers. Currently, the Llawlech ridge is covered by an access agreement through the Tir Cymen Scheme, which ends shortly. You are advised to check with the Snowdonia National Park over future access arrangements.
START Tal-y-bont [SH 589218]
DIRECTIONS See **Walk 6**.

I Follow instructions in paragraph 1 of **Walk 7** to reach Lleti Lloegr. Turn RIGHT and follow the lane down over Pont Fadog – *a stone inscription dates it 1762 and names H.Ed(ward) as the mason employed by William Vaughan of Cors y Gedol* – and continue up the lane to go through a gate at its end. *Note the nearby Scots pines – a traditional means of guiding drovers to Lleti Loegr.* Swing RIGHT along a track, and after about 25 yards at a track junction, go LEFT.

2 Follow the track up to go through a gate. The track heads east on a long gentle ascent into boulder covered upland pasture, passing through three gates. *Looking back, there are extensive views of Shell Island, Bardsey Island, the Lleyn Peninsula, and the*

central mountains of Snowdonia. The track then gently descends to go through another gate. *Just to the north is the rocky Craig y Dinas, on which is a prehistoric hillfort and settlement.* Continue with the track to skirt the north western side of Llyn Erddyn still hidden by a small rise. *A very short detour will convince you that it exists! In the mid 19thC the trout caught here before sunrise were considered to be the best in the area. It is known as the 'priest lake' from its association with Druids, who reputedly used the large stones along its banks as seats for worshipping, and kept a store of fish at its outlet.* After going through another gate the track deteriorates, but the way ahead is quite clear. *To your left is the rounded hill of Moelfre.* Up to your right is Llawlech. After a while look back to see Llyn Erddyn. After going through another gate, keep ahead, over a stream and on through the wide reedy valley – *with your first sight of Pont Scethin.* After crossing another stream you pass a small waymark post. About 75 yards beyond a second small post, you reach a broad cross path. *This is the old Harlech road.*

16

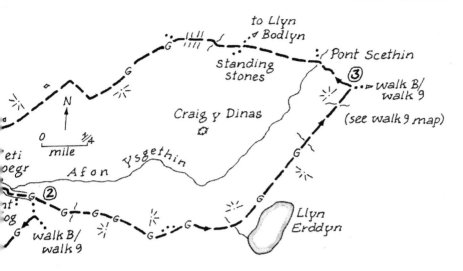

3 For **Walk B**, turn RIGHT and follow the old green road up past the memorial to the top of the bwlch by a stone cairn, gate and ladder-stile. Turn RIGHT and follow the stiled courtesy path alongside the wall on your left across the broad ridge of Llawlech up to the summit cairn and on down to Bwlch y Rhiwygr. Turn RIGHT down the pass and follow this old route, at first a path, then a green track for nearly two miles (see paragraph 3 of **Walk 9** – instructions for Walk A) passing through two gates and crossing two ladder-stiles. At a waymark post by a wall, before reaching a familiar track junction, turn LEFT to follow a green track through a gate, and on down towards a house. Turn LEFT past the facing end of a large stone barn, and on up to cross a stone stile. Follow a path leading RIGHT to pass through a wall gap, and on to cross a stile in a fence. Head towards a large building, go through a small metal gate in the wall, and follow a walled track RIGHT, down to a road. Continue down the road. After about ½ mile, at a footpath post just before Anned Wen, turn RIGHT and follow the narrow path to cross a footbridge over the river to join your outward route.

For **Walk A**, turn LEFT and follow the old road down to Pont Scethin – *an important*

crossing point of the Afon Yysgethin on this ancient road used for centuries by travellers and later drovers. Continue on the line of the old road rising steadily up the hillside. *When it levels out, look for two separate small prehistoric standing stones on your left.* At a wide track which services Llyn Bodlyn reservoir further up the valley, turn LEFT and follow the track passing beneath the southern slopes of Moelfre. *Just before it bends down to go through a gate, a metal gate on your right indicates the continuing course of the old road.* Your route continues ahead following the track on a long gentle descent – *later becoming enclosed by walls* – to reach a road.

4 Continue ahead and follow the road past numerous buildings of historic Cors y Gedol (see **Walk 7**) then Llys Faen to reach an ornate stone gateway. Continue along the straight section of road. After about 200 yards, turn LEFT through a gate by a footpath post into the wood. Keep ahead on a clear path to go through a gate and over a stream. Now bear RIGHT on a wide stony path and follow it through the wood. At a crossroad of paths, take the LEFT fork and keep with the main path to soon meet your outward route. Follow it back to the start.

WALK 9

AROUND LLAWLECH

DESCRIPTION An exhilarating 10 mile walk (**A**) for experienced walkers following delightful ancient upland trackways over two high mountain passes to complete an upland circuit around Llawlech. Starting from about 400 feet, the route crosses high upland pasture before rising steadily to Bwlch y Rhiwygr (1494 feet) at the western end of Llawlech. It descends to pass through Cwm Ysgethin on an old drovers route, then follows the other old Harlech road from near Pont Scethin up over an unnamed bwlch (1829 feet) for a superb scenic descent. Allow about 6 hours. The route also includes a 5½ mile walk (**B**) crossing the slopes of Llawlech, and a 6¼ mile walk (**C**) crossing the 1¾ mile Llawlech ridge itself (1932 feet). Currently, the ridge is covered by an access agreement through the Tir Cymen Scheme, which ends shortly. You are advised to check with the Snowdonia National Park over future access arrangements.

START Pont Hirgwm [SH 668198]

DIRECTIONS From Bontddu, by the entrance to Bontddu Hall, take a minor road angling away from the A496. Follow it up the valley to a small parking area just before the road crosses over the river (Pont Hirgwm) by a telephone box.

*Until the building of turnpike roads in the late 18th- and early 19thC, enabling good access along the Mawddach estuary and the coast, travelling and moving goods by pack horse between Harlech and Dolgellau, linking with other roads to London, required following ancient highways, possibly prehistoric in origin, across the mountains. Drovers also used these routes to move cattle from the coast near Harlech on their way to markets in England. Rising from Bontddu the ancient road divides into two branches. One (**a**) went to Harlech via Bwlch y Rhiwygr and Tal-y-Bont. The other (**b**) took a shorter more direct route, but over a higher pass, to reach Harlech via Llanbedr, and may*

have been a summer route. It is also speculated that this well constructed route is a Roman road. During the 18thC, when local gentry were becoming increasingly anglicised, the old road was an important link via Dolgellau to London Society. Inhabitants of Bontddu, would also walk part of this way on their ardous 5-mile walk via Bwlch y Llan to the 13thC parish church in Llanaber. Improvements to the old road were made in 1765 at the request of William Vaughan of Cors y Gedol. In the 18th- and early 19thC peat cut upon the mountain top was brought down the old road in trucks on sleds.

I Cross the bridge and follow the road for about ¾ mile up to its end, at a junction of paths. Here, go through a small metal gate set back on the right. Follow the path alongside the wall, then swing sharp LEFT up the hillside to reach an inscribed milestone, marking the two branches of the old road. Take the LEFT fork – Tal-y-Bont (route **a**). Follow the delightful green track up the hillside, over a ladder-stile and on down through a gate and past a ruin. *On nearby Bryn Castell is an ancient hillfort, and a medieval settlement.* The old road, marked by small white-capped posts, is easy to follow, even though it deteriorates after crossing a ladder-stile. After going through a gate, the track becomes walled and passes the ruin of Rhos caerau – *a former staging post that once provided refreshments for passing travellers.* It then passes along the edge of a replanted forest, and through a gate. At the plantation corner it goes through another gate and crosses a stream. After crossing another stream, at a white topped post, where the track bends half-left towards a gate, keep straight ahead alongside a stream to cross a stone stile in the wall and on to another stony track. *The old route to Llanaber church continued further along the valley.*

2 For **Walk A** continue ahead to follow the delightful old green track up open slopes, through a gate, and on up to the top of Bwlch y Rhiwgyr. (*For **Walk B** follow the track right, through a gate and on towards*

18

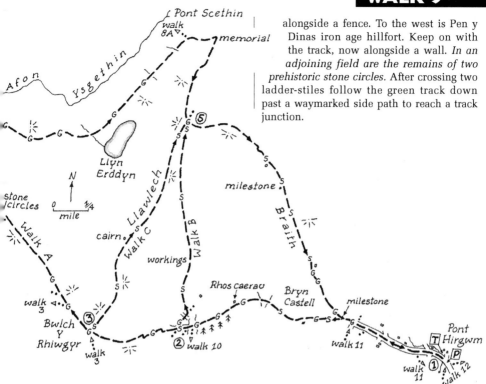

alongside a fence. To the west is Pen y Dinas iron age hillfort. Keep on with the track, now alongside a wall. *In an adjoining field are the remains of two prehistoric stone circles.* After crossing two ladder-stiles follow the green track down past a waymarked side path to reach a track junction.

a ruin. Just after crossing a second stream, head half-left up the gorse covered ground to cross a distant ladder-stile. Continue ahead up the hillside and on to pass by old workings. Now contour across the steep slopes to drop down to a wall corner. Follow the wall up to cross a ladder-stile. Now head half-left up the steep tussocky slopes, over a wall, and on up to cross a ladder-stile in the wall corner at the top of the bwlch.)

3 Go through a small gate at the top of Bwlch y Rhiwgyr. *(For Walk C, turn right and follow the stiled path alongside the wall up to the summit cairn at 1932 feet, and on across the broad level ridge to reach a small wooden gate, and stone cairn at the top of the other bwlch.)* For **Walk A** follow the path down the narrow pass. After going through a metal gate, continue ahead past side paths down to go through another gate. The path continues alongside the wall, then becomes a green track, gently descending

4 Here you leave the old Tal-y-Bont road, by turning RIGHT. Now follow a gated track for 2½ miles past Llyn Erddyn to reach the old Harlech–London road above Pont Scethin, following instructions in paragraph 2 of **Walk 8**. Then, turn RIGHT and follow the old road as it gradually rises, then angles up across the open slopes, past the Janet Haigh memorial to reach the top of the bwlch at the end of the Llawlech ridge.

5 Go through the gate and follow this superb high-level green highway across the head of the valley and down to cross a ladder-stile below where a wall blocks its progress. Follow it along Braich ridge, over a ladder-stile, past an old milestone and on over two further ladder-stiles. Go past an old metal stile and sheep folds, along a short walled section of track, and on down to reach the inscribed milestone. Follow your outward route back to the start.

19

CUTIA CHAPEL & PANORAMA WALK

DESCRIPTION A 5¾ mile **(A)** walk across upland pasture and through wooded valleys north-east of Barmouth, featuring part of an ancient upland route walked by worshippers from Bonddu to the 13thC parish church at Llanaber, an historic chapel, and great views. The route follows a scenic upland road to its end, then continues on a level section of the old church route, before descending to Cutiau, with its early 19thC chapel. It then follows a delightful old walled track across wooded slopes for a visit to the famous Panorama viewpoint. Allow about 3½ hours. A shorter 3½ mile walk **(B)** is included.

START Snowdonia National Park Panorama car park [SH 625166]

DIRECTIONS Leave Barmouth on the A496 towards Dolgellau. At the end of Porkington Terrace, just before Lawrenny Lodge, turn left up Panorama Road. Follow the road for ¾ mile to find the car park on the right.

On the wooded hillside just above the northern edge of the estuary, lies the hidden hamlet of Cutia, containing a former chapel, with an interesting history. It was built in 1806, when the Congregationalists began teaching their doctrine locally. One of its prime promoters was a Mr Evans, originally from Llangollen, who opened a school in Barmouth to teach basic education and the gospel. On Sundays, he preached in Barmouth, Cutia, and Dyffryn, a commitment which affected his health. In 1826, members of the three communities asked that he serve as their pastor. Their written request included the enticement of 'regarding your sustenance, we of Cutiau promise to collect £8 a year'. At the time the chapel contained 20 members. He was only 24 years old, when he was ordained here on 23rd May 1827. Later a new chapel was built in Barmouth, and he travelled throughout Wales, raising £300 towards its cost of £600. In 1844, the

Rev. James Jones took over, cleared the rest of the debt, and offered a bilingual service to English non-conformist visitors.

1 Continue along the road, keeping ahead at the junction (dead end sign) After crossing a cattle grid it begins to rise – *giving excellent views across to Cadair Idris, along the Mawddach estuary to the distant Arans, and later of the long ridge leading up to Dyffwys.* Continue along the open high-level road across upland pasture, passing cottages and farms. After just over 1 mile, just after passing through a gate by a stream, where the road bends left up to Sylfaen you have a choice. (For **Walk B** go through a gate on your right and down a stony track to pass along the right hand side of a large stone barn. Go through a gate at its far end to enter a field. Now follow the wall on your right, past a gate, to go through the gate facing you just beyond. Follow a path, then track down through a wood to reach a waymark post opposite a low stone stile. Turn right and resume text at point **4**.) For **Walk A** continue up the road.

2 Just before Sylfaen farm, at a footpath post, bear LEFT on a stony track. Follow it through a gateway and on past a small quarry. After a gate, the level track now becomes the old church route as it crosses the expansive upland pasture, passing the remains of Golodd below – *said to be where drovers left their cattle* – and then a ruined stone barn. At a junction of stony tracks keep ahead. At a stream just before a gate in the wall ahead, with a green track rising left up *the hillside (the old mountain road via Bwlch y Rhiwgyr to Tal-y-bont)*, turn RIGHT to cross a stone stile. Walk alongside the stream and on along the stony track.

3 After crossing a stream, turn RIGHT along a green track, passing a large stone enclosure, to go through a gate in the wall corner. Follow a faint green track alongside the wall to go through a gate in the corner. Bear LEFT to follow the green track to a waymarked path junction. Go through the large metal gate ahead and follow a green track alongside the edge of the forest – *soon* with views down to Barmouth bridge, and Fairbourne beyond – to reach a lane. Continue down the lane. The ruin on your right is said to be an old drover's inn. Take the second waymarked path on the right, through a gate, and follow the access track into a wooded valley, over the river, and up to Tyddyn Pandy. Pass in front of the house, then swing RIGHT, then LEFT to pass behind a stone barn. About 50 yards further, at a large tree in a low wall, go half-LEFT to work your way through a narrow field to go through a small wall gap in the bottom corner. Follow the wall on your right to cross a ladder-stile into a forest. Follow the path, then track, down through the forest to cross a low stone stile onto a green track. Continue ahead on a waymarked path.

4 Follow the green track through an area of mixed woodland, crossing three ladder-stiles, then across a more open woodland area, containing young trees of the newly created Coed y Tyn Llidiart. At a path junction by yellow marker posts, drop down LEFT and follow the path to pass between a house and Cutia chapel, now privately owned. Walk along a narrow walled driveway and on down the narrow lane past a garage. It bends left past a small roadside ruin. – said to have been a shop.

5 When the lane bends down sharp left, with a white metal gate ahead by a telegraph pole, turn RIGHT to follow a delightful narrow walled track through Coed Glan-y-Mawddach. It was part of the 17thC Dolgellau to Barmouth road, used by travellers before the building of the turnpike road, now the A496. At a waymarked path junction, go up the RIGHT fork. This delightful path, later walled again, rises steadily through the trees. After a while you will see below the ruin of Bwlch-y-Goedleoedd, reputed to be an old inn. The great 14thC Welsh poet, Dafydd ap Gwilym apparently stayed here. It is said that after his plan to meet twelve local young women at different times was discovered, he

gladly retreated to his locked room at the inn! A little further on you reach the gated entrance to the Panorama Walk. Complete the short circuit to enjoy the stunning views, then continue along the walled path to emerge from the wood. Follow the path to Panorama Road by the start.

CWM DWYNANT & COED FARCHYNYS

DESCRIPTION A 5¾ mile walk exploring the foothills and quiet upland valleys on the northern side of the Mawddach estuary just west of Bontddu, once searched for gold. Allow about 4 hours. From the car park, as an extension or a separate short walk, you can also follow the paths created by the SNP Authority to explore the attractive predominantly oak woodland of Coed Farchynys and visit the edge of the estuary.

START Snowdonia National Park Farchynys car park. [SH 662186]

DIRECTIONS Leave Barmouth on the A496 towards Dolgellau, and just before you reach Bontddu, the car park is set back on the right.

I Return to the A496 and cross the road. Turn LEFT, and after about 150 yards take a path angling up past a bridleway sign to go through a gate into a forest. Follow the bridleway rising steadily across the tree-covered slope, soon alongside a wall. At its corner keep ahead up a forestry track. After about 75 yards leave the track to continue up the bridleway to eventually leave the forest by a small wooden gate – *with views along the estuary to the railway viaduct, and Fairbourne.* Continue ahead alongside a wall. *Shortly, look back for a view of Cadair Idris.* The bridleway now bends north across *the rhodendrum, bracken, gorse, and heather covered slopes. Below is Caerdeon church, built in 1862 in the style of an Italian hillside chapel for private use, and consecrated as a church in 1887.* After a while you reach a large stone wall on the left.

2 Here, go through the larger of two wooden gates, and on along a short section of walled bridleway. After crossing a stream, continue up by a wall, and on up a stony track to a lane. Follow it RIGHT, soon passing the entrance to Bwlch-yr-ysgol. Shortly,

at a waymarked path junction, by a large stone, turn LEFT and follow a forestry road, soon alongside a narrow section of oak trees on your right. Just before their end, at a waymark post, take the path angling down and follow it near a wall beneath the forest. Just beyond the wall corner, at a waymark post, you have a choice. (*For a shorter walk turn right down through the conifers to cross a ladder-stile. Go along a green track, and at a wooden gate, turn left down an old walled section of path and through a small gate. Keep on with the path, through a metal gate, then swing left between a house and outbuilding to cross over the Afon Dwynant to reach a lane. Turn right and resume text at point 3.*) For the main route continue ahead on a gradual descent through the forest edge to reach a green track by farm buildings. Follow it down past the farmhouse and on down its access track to the lane. Turn RIGHT and follow it along the attractive Cwm Dwynant for nearly ½ mile to pass a telephone box.

3 Continue up the lane, then take the RIGHT fork. Follow this delightful narrow lane up the side of Cwm Dwynant, passing Cae-mur Hywel – *near which was a trial for gold in 1862.* Just past Capel Moriah, go half-LEFT to a fence corner. Now follow the fence on your right, then a wall, to pass between conifers to reach Caegwian. Here, turn LEFT up a track, and at a track junction, keep ahead. At the next track junction, by a waymark post, take the RIGHT fork. *Nearby was a small and unsuccessful 1850s gold mine.* Soon you leave the mixed woodland by a gate. Continue on the track. *Ahead is the dome-shaped Bryn Castell, on which is an ancient hillfort, and a medieval settlement.* Cross over the river, and just past an outbuilding, opposite Bwthyn Bach, turn LEFT and follow a meandering green track. When it bends left towards a stone building, turn RIGHT to drop down through a line of trees and across a reedy area to the wall above a cottage. Here, turn LEFT and go through a gate in the wall corner. Go across the field to cross a ladder-stile above a cottage, and on across the next field to cross another ladder-stile. Go across Gwyliwch-y-ci's access track

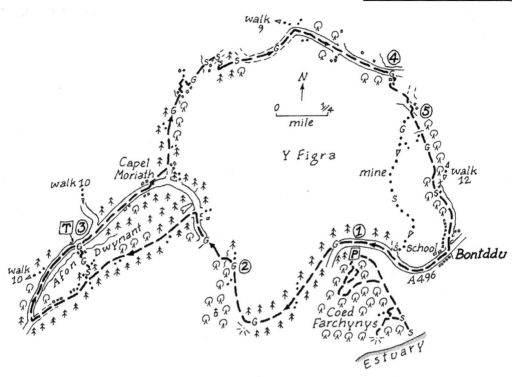

to cross a stile ahead. Bear RIGHT, then LEFT alongside a wall. After about 15 yards, turn LEFT and follow a path up through the trees to soon leave the wood by a stile. Follow the nearby access track to reach the end of a road. Go down the road – *enjoying views of Diffwys to the north and Cadair Idris to the south east* – past the entrance to Cae Hir, and Cae Goronwy. *Ahead on Clogau mountain can be seen evidence of gold-mining – waste tips, and an incline across the slopes.*

4 About 200 yards below Tynlon Uchaf, when close above the river, turn RIGHT through a recessed gate, and on to bear LEFT round the side and end of an outbuilding. Go through a gate just before another small building and through the open gateway ahead. After a few yards, turn LEFT to follow a green track down the narrow raised field. At an access track, go half-RIGHT on a waymarked path to follow another track past a barn. Just before a stream, drop down LEFT and on through a waymarked wall gap. Cross the stream and follow a green track through a gap in the wall. (*For an alternative high-level route via the disused Figra mine as shown on the map, turn right up near the wall. At the time of writing the descent path from the mine was awaiting some clearance work.*)

5 Continue along the soon descending track, then after crossing a stream, follow a waymarked path angling off the rising track down a field to go through a small gate in the left-hand corner. Follow the path along the top edge of the narrow wooded valley. At a wall corner, keep ahead to go through an area of gorse, then bracken, to pass between two concrete supports. Drop down the incline and at a fence bear RIGHT to follow a path down to cross a ladder-stile near the site of Figra Mill (See **Walk 12**). Continue ahead and follow a broad track down past Hirgwn gorge, then a lane to the A496. Turn RIGHT and follow the road through Bontddu back to the start.

ABOVE BONTDDU

DESCRIPTION A 3 mile walk (**A**) tracing some of the area's gold mining history. The route takes you up the impressive wooded Hirgwm gorge, past the site of Figra Mill and the entrance to Clogau gold mine up to Pont Hirgwm. It then visits an important mine adit before rising across the upland pasture of Clogau mountain to a higher level mine at just over 800 feet. It descends a delightful green tramway then lane, before finishing by the Hirgwm gorge. Allow about 2 hours. The route can easily be shortened to a 1¼ mile walk (**B**).

START Old bridge over Afon Hirgwm, Bontddu [SH 669187]

DIRECTIONS Leave Barmouth on the A496 towards Dolgellau to reach Bontddu. After passing the school and a garage take a turning on the left. Immediately turn right over the river and park tidily. Alternative roadside parking is available further along the A496 on the right.

The steep-sided Hirgwm Valley and surrounding hills once echoed to the sound of mining, becoming one of the most important gold-mining areas in Britain. Small-scale mining, primarily for copper and lead, probably occurred here since before the Romans. Between 1825-45, Figra and Old Clogau mines, on opposite sides of the valley, were worked for copper. But a chance discovery of gold, worth thousand of pounds, on a spoil tip in 1854 led to the first of several gold rushes. The working of the gold bearing quartz veins, primarily the St. David's Lode, during the rest of the century, in what became known as the Clogau Mine, was undertaken by a series of companies, some shortlived. A gold rush in 1862 saw the existing company awarded a medal at the Great Exhibition. From 1898 to the early 1900s, mining was larger in scale, involving up to 63 men working above ground and 190 below, and producing a peak yield of 18,417 oz of gold in 1904. Mining has con-

tinued intermittingly since then, producing the famous Clogau gold used to make wedding rings for the Royal Family. Most gold extraction involved adit mining - inclined tunnels driven by hand until the 1870s when compressed-air drills were introduced. They provided access to the ore, drainage and ventilation.

Figra Mill, powered by a waterwheel, was built as a crushing mill to serve the copper mines, then adapted for gold production in 1862. A zig-zag track and incline connected the mill with Figra mine above. There were constant changes in machinery to improve the extraction of gold from pulverised quartz and reduce the gold being lost in the process. Mechanical crushing was done by 'stamps', heavy columns of wood and iron, requiring massive foundations and reinforcement of the river bank. At the end of the 19thC a new mill powered by a turbine was built, with a gas engine as standby. Just downstream was a smaller mill in use until the 1930s, whose Britten pans used mercury to extract the fine gold particles. In the 1890s high grade ore was brought here in locked boxes by Robin the donkey!

I After crossing the old bridge, turn RIGHT up a lane passing beneath houses, then continue along a track above the impressive deep wooded river gorge. Soon you pass the remains of Figra mill to cross Figra Bridge. Bear LEFT up the path, past a track leading to houses. After a few yards, leave the stony track to follow a path closer to the river, soon rising through delightful woodland to rejoin the track. Shortly you reach the secured entrance to Clogau mine – first worked in 1862, and connected by Llechfraith adit to the main workings on Clogau mountain in 1903. Follow the path, through a gate, and up across open slopes to go through a kissing gate onto a road near Pont Hirgwm. (*For* **Walk B** *turn right along the road to point* **4**.)

2 Go through the large gate opposite, and walk along the track. Just before reaching a farm head half-RIGHT up the hillside, through a gap in the wall, then follow the wall on the left to cross a fence/wall in the field corner (stile to be installed). Drop down the slope to join a track at the end of its long stone barn. When it splits keep to the RIGHT fork for a short diversion. Pass above a ruin, and by a waste tip to reach a small stone building by the gated entrance to the Ty'n-y-cornel adit. *Started in 1880 and reaching 1102 ft by the end of 1881, and extended by a new company between 1888-90, it cost consider-able effort and money, but for little return. Businessmen from Barmouth then profited from this hugh capi-tal investment, employing about 25 men between 1891-98. Under a new company, between 1898-1903, as the workings were being extended, and the Llechfraith adit being dug, ore was transported from the adit mouth in 6 cwt buckets on a 1,100 yards aerial ropeway dropping 210 ft down to Figra Mill.* Return to where the track splits. Instead, head north near the wall on your left to cross the wall ahead in the corner (stone stile to be installed). Continue ahead to follow the wall on your left.

3 When you reach a wall up on your right with a faint green track ahead, swing sharp RIGHT up alongside the wall, soon on a path. At the wall corner containing a small ruin – *with a good view of Diffwys* – go half-RIGHT and follow the path up the hillside and through a gate. Keep ahead to join another path by the wall on your right. Follow this path back to cross the ladder-stile. *Nearby is a tip and drain-age adit for one of two new mines worked in the late 1850s/early 1860s. On top of the mountain is the Old Clogau copper and gold mine. By 1865, a system of tramways and inclines were being built around the moun-tain to transport ore down to Figra Mill.* Turn RIGHT and follow the old tramway through two gates. Keep on with this delightful level green tramway. At a waymark post, when the tramway splits, go down the RIGHT fork and through a kissing gate. Continue with the old tramway down the hillside, passing through a large gate. When it levels out, just before a cottage, swing sharp RIGHT down a path to join the road by another cottage. Turn LEFT down the road.

4 At a footpath post, turn RIGHT down a track past cottages to join your outward route. Turn LEFT down the path. Just before Figra bridge, keep straight ahead on a nar-row path to go through a kissing gate. Follow the path through the wood, over a stream, soon dropping down to go through another kissing gate. Just below, take the lower path above Hirgwm gorge on through the trees to go through a small gate to pass down the side of a house and former chapel to the road near the start.

CWM GWYNANT & LLYNNAU CREGENNAN

DESCRIPTION This highly scenic 8 mile walk takes you through an outstandingly beautiful area on the southern side of the Mawddach estuary, offering superb views. The route follows nearly 3 miles of the Mawddach Trail on the former Ruabon railway line along the wooded edge of the estuary, before heading inland up the attractive wooded Cwm Gwynant past King's Youth Hostel. It then passes along a wide upland valley below the Cadair Idris range to the beautiful Cregennan lakes, before descending in stages to Arthog. Allow about 4½ hours.
START Lay-by beneath Arthog village hall [SH 637141] or Snowdonia National Park Arthog car park [SH 640148]
DIRECTIONS See **Walk 14**.

It is hard to believe that to-day's tranquil estuary was once a hive of activity. Its creeks supported numerous shipyards attracted by the plentiful local oak, and between 1750 – 1865 some 318 vessels were launched on the Mawddach. There was also a flourishing trade in imported goods such as lime, coal, sugar, soap and candles, and in the export of woollen 'webs' , a coarse white cloth woven locally, and later, timber and slate. From 1869 steam trains ran regulary along the estuary on the Ruabon-Barmouth railway bringing many visitors into the area. As late as the 1950s, on Saturdays in summer, trains from different parts of England, full of passengers, many bound for Butlins in Pwllheli, passed this way. The line closed in 1965.

I Cross the road, and turn RIGHT to walk along the grass verge. Shortly, at a footpath post, turn LEFT and follow the path through two gates to reach the Mawddach Trail. Turn RIGHT and follow the Trail past the site of the former Arthog Station, now the SNP car park, over a bridge and on along the side of the estuary. *On the left is a saltmarsh*

– an important wildlife site for waders. The demand for housing slate led to several quarries being opened in the hills adjoining the estuary. The visible Ty'n y Coed quarry operated between 1860 and the early 1880s, when high costs forced its closure. Eventually you reach the information board at the former Garth Siding, where once stood two cottages for railwaymen. *Finished slate travelled from the cutting shed in trucks down an incline and along a tramway, to be taken away by sailing boat from a nearby jetty. Later it was taken from here by train.* Continue ahead, past the remains of the old jetty and tramway. After a while, the estuary narrows – *where the clash between an incoming tide and the river is more evident* - then widens again. Eventually you reach an information board at Abergwynant.

2 Just after passing over the Afon Gwynant, swing sharp RIGHT down a stony track and follow it near the river along the edge of Abergwynant Wood. Just beyond a small pool bear RIGHT through a gate, soon following an access track by the river and keep ahead up the lane to reach the A493. Cross the road, turn LEFT, then go up a side road. Follow this quiet road up the attractive wooded Gwynant valley close by the river for 1 mile to reach King's Youth hostel. Continue up the road and on the bend, follow the waymarked path through a small gate and up through the wood to rejoin the road by a small ruined chapel and neat graveyard, still used to-day. Continue along the road and when it bends over the river, keep ahead along a green track to enter open country. Continue on the track towards a large stone house – *with good views south east to Cadair Idris*. When the track fades, keep ahead to follow a waymarked path through an old gateway. Go up a field, through another gateway, and on up to go through a small metal gate by a stream.

3 Continue up the path, which soon heads west along the wide upland valley by the nearby Cadair Idris range, passing beneath Craggy Pared y Cefn hir – *on which is a Romano British hillfort*. After a while the larger of the Cregennan lakes appears

gaps to cross a ladder-stile. Turn RIGHT and follow the waymarked path across the gorse covered slope, through another wall gap and on over a ladder-stile. Go on to pass through a wall gap into a walled track. Turn LEFT, and just beyond its end, turn RIGHT and walk along the field edge past a ruin, and on with a stony track. Keep on through a gate ahead to follow another track. Soon take a path angling down to cross a delightful old stone clapper bridge. *Nearby upstream is the site of Llys Bradwen, reputed to have been the court of Bradwen, leader of one of the fifteen tribes of North Wales in the early 12thC.* Turn RIGHT along a green track up to a road. Continue down the road past Cregennan Farm. At a bend go through a gate marked Tyn-y-grai. Follow the stony track, go through another gate and on past Merddyn cottage. Follow the gated path on a steady descent to reach a lane beneath Arthog village hall. Turn RIGHT down to the start.

ahead. Near the lake, at a waymark post, turn LEFT on the National Trust path. At a waymarked junction, bear RIGHT near the lake edge to cross two stiles. Turn LEFT and follow the waymarked path soon by the edge of the second lake to cross a ladder-stile by a boathouse. Turn RIGHT and follow the path up by the wall and on to reach a road. Turn RIGHT and follow it by the lake, past a car park and toilets – *soon with stunning views down to Barmouth bridge.* Follow the highly scenic road meandering down the hillside, past a ruined cottage then Cefn-hir-isaf.

4 When the road bends right by a footpath post, keep ahead up the open hillside alongside a wall. Follow the waymarked path bearing half-LEFT through two wall

27

ARTHOG FALLS & LLYNNAU CREGENNAN

DESCRIPTION A 6½ mile (**A**) or 4 mile (**B**) walk, exploring the tremendously varied beautiful lowland and upland scenery around Arthog, offering stunning views. The route initially crosses and meanders round Arthog Bog, an SSSI, briefly visiting the edge of the Mawddach Estuary, then follows the Afon Arthog up a narrow wooded gorge past waterfalls to a clapper bridge near the medieval site of Llys Bradwen. The main route extends on an upland circuit to visit one of the beautiful Cregennan lakes, owned by the National Trust. The joint route then crosses upland pasture, before descending through attractive woodland to a RSPB Nature Reserve, and on along a short section of the Mawddach Trail. Allow about 4½ hours for the main route.

START Lay-by beneath Arthog Village Hall [SH 637141] or Snowdonia National Park Arthog car park [SH 640148]

DIRECTIONS Travelling on the A493 from Friog towards Dolgellau you will find the lay-by on the right at the western end of Arthog. For the SNP car park proceed further along the road, and just past Arthog Terrace, built in the 1860's, turn left by a green corrugated building on a side road signposted Min-y- Don.

I From the lay-by beneath the Village Hall, cross the road and turn RIGHT along the grass verge. Shortly, turn LEFT down a waymarked path, and follow it through two gates to reach the Mawddach Trail. Go through the gate ahead, and on with the path across Arthog Bog. *It contains many uncommon grasses and plants, attracting birds and butterflies. In the past, peat was dug up and taken away in sailing boats to be used as fuel.* Soon you reach a gate overlooking the estuary – *with views across to Barmouth.* Turn RIGHT through an adjoining gate, and follow the path – *with views*

of the Cadair Idris range – to reach a lane. Here, turn RIGHT along the waymarked path across the gorse, reed, and shrub covered terrain towards the distant Arthog Terrace, soon bearing half-LEFT to go on to reach a road. Turn RIGHT and follow it over the Mawddach Trail, by the SNP car park on the site of the former Arthog Station.

2 Continue along the road by a small inlet – *with the castellated 17thC Arthog Hall prominent on the wooded hillside.* Shortly cross a ladder-stile on the left and follow the path, soon alongside the Afon Arthog, to reach the A493. Turn LEFT, then go through a small gate on the right opposite St. Catherine's Church. Follow the path rising steadily up the wooded side valley above the river. About 25 yards after an old gateway, take a smaller side path on the right. It rises through the trees, soon alongside the river cascading down a narrow rocky gorge. Just before small falls, the path bends sharp right up away from the river, then continues along the top edge of the wooded valley. After crossing a ladder-stile the path continues above the higher falls, soon close by the river to eventually level out. Cross a ladder-stile to reach a green track near a delightful stone clapper bridge. (*For* **Walk B**, *follow instructions from point* **4**.) Cross over this bridge, and on with the path to join a track. *Nearby to your right is the site of two adjoining medieval buildings, known as Llys Bradwen, reputed to have been the court of Bradwen, leader of one of the 15 tribes of North Wales in the early 12thC.* Follow the track through a gate and on up to a wall corner.

3 Here, continue ahead on the waymarked path along the field edge, past a ruin, then swing LEFT to go between two walls. Go through a gap in the wall on your right and on to cross a ladder-stile. Follow the waymarked path across the craggy gorse-covered upland pasture – *with extensive views across the estuary to Barmouth and the Lleyn peninsular, and to the southern Rhinogs* – through a wall gap, and over a ladder-stile just beyond a ruin. Go half-RIGHT down the waymarked path, through two wall gaps, and on down the field edge to follow the road

ladder-stile ahead. Continue up alongside the wall and on over a ladder-stile in the corner – *with new views to Fairbourne and the coast*. Go down the field, over another ladder-stile, then go half-LEFT to pass through a derelict upland farm. Bear RIGHT to go through a gate, and on along its green access track. When it bends left by a roof-

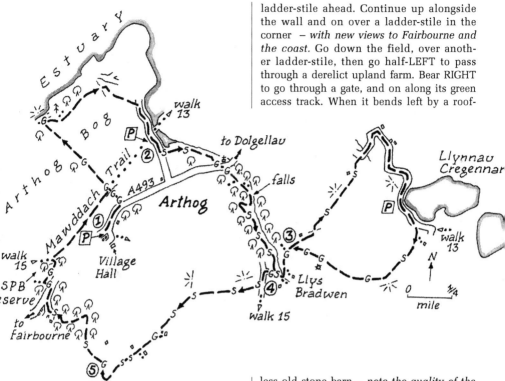

ahead. It rises steadily up the attractive hillside to suddenly arrive at the stunning sight of the larger of the Cregennan lakes – *part of an estate, gifted to the Trust in 1959*. Follow the road past a National Trust car park and toilets. Shortly, take a waymarked path on the right, soon passing to the right of a small rocky hillock, then marshy area to cross a stone stile. Go along the field edge, then follow the path angling away from the wall onto a small rise. Continue down the path to go through a gate by a footpath post. Follow a green track down to another footpath post, then bear RIGHT to follow the wall along the edge of three fields – *passing a small group of prehistoric stones in an adjoining field* – to join your outward route back over the clapper bridge.

4 Turn RIGHT up the green track, then LEFT along a road. Shortly, cross a stile on your right, go up the field and over a

less old stone barn – *note the quality of the stonework* – continue ahead on a waymarked path, over a stile in the fence, and on over a ladder-stile. Keep ahead along the field edge, and at a stile on the left, before a stream, turn RIGHT down rough pasture.

5 At a waymark post in a section of wall, go RIGHT alongside the boundary. After going through a gateway, turn LEFT to reach a wall end. Drop down the open slope, then bear RIGHT on a clear path, over a stile, and on down through attractive woodland – *full of bluebells in Spring*. After crossing a ladder-stile at the bottom of the wood by a house, go down its driveway to the A493. Go along the road and shortly go through a kissing gate on the left to enter Arthog Bog RSPB Nature Reserve. After about 25 yards, turn RIGHT on a side path, and follow it past an information board to join the tree-lined Mawddach Trail. Turn RIGHT and follow it to the cross-path of your outward route. Follow it back to the start.

BENEATH CRAIG CWM-LLWYD

DESCRIPTION A 5½ mile walk exploring the attractive foothills lying south of Morfa Mawddach, offering panoramic views. Initially, the route follows the Mawddach Trail before rising steadily up through the hills above Arthog to join a short section of the scenic high-level Ffordd Ddu ancient trackway (See **Walk 19**) beneath the rocky escarpment of Craig Cwm-llwyd, reaching a height of over 1100 feet, before descending to pass 18thC Cyfanned Fawr and a nearby 19thC silver-lead mine. Allow about 4 hours.
START Morfa Mawddach Halt [SH 628141]
DIRECTIONS About 1 mile east of Friog, by a war memorial, turn off the A493 signposted to the railway halt at Morfa Mawddach, where there is a car park and toilets.

Morfa Mawddach, known as Barmouth Junction until 1960, was once one of the busiest junctions in mid-Wales, offering through services to London, the Midlands and the North. Often Welsh singing could be heard here, so popular did its two refreshment rooms become with the local people!

I Join the Mawddach Trail by the toilet block, and follow it through the trees, over a lane, and on through a metal gate. Continue along the tree-lined Trail, passing an RSPB Nature Reserve site. After a further ⅓ mile, at a clear cross-path, turn RIGHT and follow the path to the A493. Turn RIGHT along the grass verge. Shortly, just before the lay-by, take the lane on the left angling up towards the Village Hall. On the bend turn LEFT up a path and on through two small gates. Follow the path up through the edge of the wood through another gate, and on more steeply up the wooded hillside, passing a side path to Buarth. The gradient then eases and soon you pass Merddyn cottage to follow a stone track to a road. Continue up the road past Cregennan farm, *a seat offering extensive views*, and a green track, to a road junction. (Turning right offers an alternative scenic ancient upland road to point **3**.)

2 Go through the gate ahead and follow the superb walled green track up the hillside to go through a gate to join Ffordd Ddu. Continue up this stonier track and through another gate. The track crosses, then rises steadily up the wild upland slopes beneath rocky Craig Cwm-llwyd – offering panoramic views. At a footpath post, leave the track and follow the path alongside the wall – *soon passing a plaque recording the Americans who were tragically killed on their way home on the 8th June 1945* – to cross a stile. Now follow the clear path – *a link to a lower ancient highway* – down and across the high upland pasture, through a gate by a stream, and on to cross a stile by the corner of a plantation. *In the nearby clearing is an old hut circle settlement.* Follow a green track through the plantation down to reach a lane.

3 Go through the kissing gate just below and follow a track round past Cyfanned Fawr. *This imposing quality stone building, dating from 1748, was once a house of some importance. In the middle of the last century, it was occupied by Morus Jones, a well known poet and winner of many bardic chairs.* After passing a large outbuilding, at a waymarked path junction, follow a delightful walled green track heading towards Barmouth to descend the hillside. This was part of the old upland road network leading down to Friog. *On your left are the remains of an old mine, first opened in 1827, but mainly worked between 1851-63, producing lead, cop-*

per and silver. Lead ore was taken to Penrhyn Point and by ferry to Barmouth from where it was shipped to Swansea for smelting and refining. In the 1880s it was worked for slate. The track passes along the edge of a small wood and continues down to a large gate. Go through a kissing gate above this gate and follow the part stony path down through an area of open birch, soon bending LEFT down to join another path.

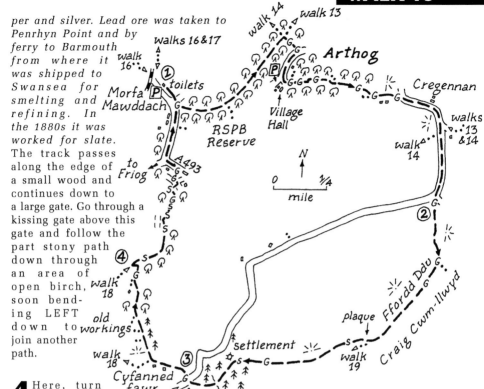

4 Here, turn sharp RIGHT and follow the path to cross a ladder-stile. Continue along the bottom edge of a wood. *Between the mid-1860's and 1873, slate was extracted from nearby Tyddyn Sieffre quarries, by companies which both went into liquidation.* Cross another ladder-stile by a small clearing. Keep ahead to go through a gap in the gorse corner, and just before a gate on a track, turn RIGHT to follow a path alongside the boundary. Cross a ladder-stile, and keep on with the enclosed path, over another ladder-stile, and on through a kissing-gate to drop down steps into a field. Go down the slope, soon following a path down through the trees past a small old quarry, over a ladder-stile and on down to join a track by a house. Follow it LEFT, and at the track junction, go through a kissing-gate, and follow a path down to the A493 by Glasfryn Terrace. Turn LEFT along the road – *passing a garage bearing the old Arthog railway halt sign* – and at the war memorial, turn RIGHT and follow the road back to the start. *Your return route follows the line of a 3 foot gauge tramway built in 1899, by the entrepreneur Solomon Andrews from Tyddyn Shieffrey tips to Morfa Mawddach, initially to carry quarry waste and materials for the building of houses. like Glasfryn and St. Mary's Crescent, and roads. It was part of a network of tramways built to help realise his ambitious but unfulfilled plans for developing the area into a holiday resort (see* **Walk 16**).

31

BARMOUTH BRIDGE

DESCRIPTION A 3¾ mile walk, with superb views, over the magnificent 19thC rail and toll footbridge across the tidal mouth of the Mawddach estuary, following the Mawddach Trail on the former railway line to Ruabon, to visit Arthog Bog Nature Reserve. Allow about 2 hours.

START Harbour, Barmouth [SH 616154]

The railway viaduct stretching for ½ mile across the mouth of the estuary is one of the wonders of Wales. Built in 1867 it consists of 113 spans supported by over 500 timber piles. Its original 'drawbridge' over the navigation channel was replaced in 1899 by the current steel swing bridge, which requires eight men to operate manually. For a few months as the bridge was nearing completion, passengers were taken over the bridge in a carriage drawn by two horses. This must have been quite a sight! The railway gave local people access to various parts of Britain, and brought in many middle class Victorian visitors. Thankfully the bridge has survived closure threats, notably in 1980 from damage caused by the teredo worm.

I Follow the nearby main road out of Barmouth towards Dolgellau. At Porkington Terrace (1870), take the pathway opposite down past the Lifeboat Station to the bridge toll booth. Go across the bridge – enjoying the extensive views – and through a gate at the far end. Continue on the path alongside the railway and through another gate. *Near a small gate on the left, once stood a refreshment and waiting room built in 1899 at the start of a horse-drawn tramway – still visible. Both were part of ambitious plans by Solomon Andrews, a remarkable self-made businessman, to develop the nearby area into a resort as he had at Pwllheli. The tramway took visitors to the estuary, then in 1903, on a circuit of Fegla Fawr, passing the three-storey Mawddach Crescent he had built. After then his plans came to an end.* Continue

past Morfa Mawddach halt and toilets on the Mawddach Trail and over a lane.

2 Go through a metal gate, and on along the tree-lined Trail, then take a way-marked RSPB path on the right to enter Arthog Bog Nature Reserve. Follow the path through the trees, a gate, and on to reach a cross-path. Here, turn RIGHT and follow the path to the road. Turn RIGHT past St. Mary's Crescent and on back to Morfa Mawddach halt, before making another enjoyable crossing over Barmouth bridge.

THE MOUTH OF THE MAWDDACH

DESCRIPTION An unusual 3½ mile walk that starts with a ferry crossing and features two living pieces of railway history and great views. The route takes the ferry across to Porth Penrhyn – the terminus of the Fairbourne and Barmouth narrow gauge steam railway – then heads towards Fairbourne, before taking an embanked path across the salt-marsh edges to Morfa Mawddach. It then returns by the historic railway/toll bridge across the estuary. Allow about 2½ hours. The walk can be combined with a railway trip into Fairbourne to visit the free railway museum and nature centre, or to the intermediate station with the world's longest name. *Note the ferry operates from April to September and is subject to tide and weather.*

START Harbour, Barmouth [SH 616154]

From earliest times a ferry has provided an important link between settlements. Once it was run by local monks from Ynys y Brawd, then a small island. After the Reformation it was run by local fishermen. In the 19thC, it was owned by the Barmouth Harbour Trust, and Penrhyn Farm on Porth Penrhyn played a key role in its operation. There were two boats, one for passengers, and the other for animals, wheeled vehicles, general goods

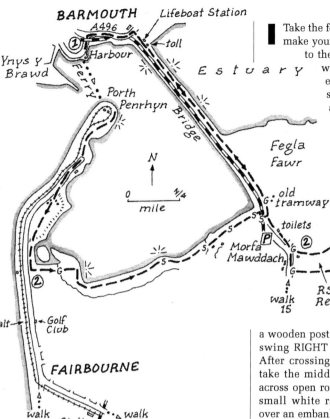

BARMOUTH Lifeboat Station

A496

toll

Harbour

Ynys y Brawd

Estuary

Porth Penrhyn

Bridge

Fegla Fawr

N

0 ¼ mile

old tramway

toilets

Morfa Mawddach

walks 14 & 15

walk 14

RSPB Reserve

walk 15

Golf Club

FAIRBOURNE

walk 18 Station walk 18

I Take the ferry over to Porth Penrhyn and make your way up the sand and shingle to the Pavilion Restaurant and railway ticket office. Walk along the edge of the eastern shore, past a small signal box and on along a stony track by sand dunes to reach a road by a railway tunnel. Walk along the road past an emergency telephone. *On your left is the ruin of 'The Bungalow'. It was converted from outbuildings of Penrhyn Farm by Arthur McDougal to provide accommodation for his wife, but was abandoned after she had a frightening experience there one night.* Just beyond, at a wooden post, drop down off the road, then swing RIGHT along a path near the road. After crossing the end of an embankment, take the middle of three wide green paths across open rough pasture towards a distant small white railway building, later going over an embankment by a small tidal inlet to reach the road by the building.

2 Here turn LEFT past a footpath post, and go along the broad embankment by the nearby golf course – *built as part of McDougal's unfulfilled grandiose plan to develop Fairbourne into an elite resort. The grass-topped stone embankment, built in the 19thC as a sea defence, divides the extensive salt-marsh from land reclaimed to provide pasture for cattle and sheep, and later for the building of Fairbourne.* Follow the embanked path to eventually reach the mainline railway at Morfa Mawddach. Heed the warning signs before crossing the line, and go through a gate opposite. Turn LEFT and follow the path alongside the railway line and on over the railway/toll bridge, past the lifeboat station to reach the A496. Follow the road LEFT back into Barmouth.

and the Royal Mail. *Inevitably, traffic greatly decreased with the arrival of the railway in 1867. In the 20thC, the ferrymen came to rely upon the Fairbourne narrow gauge railway for a living.*

The famous 2½ mile Fairbourne railway originates from a 2 ft gauge horse drawn tramway built by Arthur McDougal (of flour fame) in 1895, initially for transporting materials for the building of Fairbourne, but extended to the ferry between 1897-98 and used to carry summer visitors. In 1916 the tramway was sold and converted into a miniature steam railway, which opened in 1919. Since then it has had a chequered history, experiencing many changes of ownership, periods of prosperity and decay, and severe flooding damage. But it has survived into the 21stC and continues to delight passengers to-day as the original tramway did in the late 1890s!

33

WALK 18
ABOVE FRIOG

DESCRIPTION A 4 mile walk exploring the valleys and hills above Friog, with great views, and finishing with a fine stretch of coast. The route, which is accessible by train and bus, leaves Fairbourne to head up the Panteinion valley to follow an ancient route rising to about 750 feet, from where it descends past old slate quarries to Friog. The route then passes through the village and returns by Fairbourne Beach. Allow about 3 hours. By using the road through Friog, the route can easily be undertaken as two separate circuits: a Fairbourne walk of 2 miles and an inland walk of 2½ miles starting from Friog.

START Fairbourne Station [SH 614129]

DIRECTIONS Turn off the A 493 into Fairbourne. After crossing the main railway line, turn right to a car park and toilets by shops.

Friog was originally a farming community that later developed through the working of two adjacent slate quarries on the southern side of the narrow Panteinion valley, opened by Dr. George Walker (1807-1884), a Nottinghamshire surgeon, renowned as a sanitary reformer. Interestingly, his gravestone in the Quaker burial ground at Bryn Tallwyn, Llwyngwil acknowledges his role in providing employment for many local people for nearly a quarter of a century. Henddol operated between 1865-71, and was later reworked in 1883. The Goleuwern quarry was opened in 1867, employing 51 men by 1872, the highest paid being the masons, then the blacksmiths, then labourers. Slate was brought down a long incline to the valley road, then taken by cart to the ferry. From the early 1890s, both quarries operated under one company, employing over 80 men. They finally closed in the late 1920s.

In the quarry, which is privately owned, is the 'blue lake', which featured in local tourist brochures. It is a 40 ft deep quarry pit that was deliberately filled with water in 1901 by Arthur McDougal's engineer to be used as a reservoir in a scheme for providing

Fairbourne with electric lighting. Pipes were laid but the scheme progressed no further.

1 Cross the railway line and follow the road out of Fairbourne to the A493. Turn RIGHT and just past the garage, turn LEFT into Ffordd yr Ysgol. After about 80 yards, turn RIGHT at a footpath sign and follow the path up alongside the school fence, through a kissing gate, and on up through the trees. Go through a small gate and on up the path - with the quarries visible ahead. After going through an old gateway, turn RIGHT towards houses. Go through a gate and on to swing LEFT between a house and large outbuilding. Go through a kissing gate and on across the access track to pass between a small stone barn and a caravan. Go past a modern barn, then just beyond its end, go half-RIGHT down a path through the trees. Follow it down to a lane by the river. Turn LEFT up the lane past a narrow waterfall on the bend – called 'Henddol Fall' in an 1863 guide.

2 Just before Panteinion Farm, at a footpath post, swing sharp RIGHT through a gate and on up a track to pass above the farm. After going through a kissing gate follow the path by the fence along the edge of the valley. This delightful green path – *a branch of the higher ancient mountain road network* – then begins to rise. When it splits, go up the RIGHT fork. Follow it up and go through a hidden kissing gate above a large gate. Continue ahead, taking the LEFT fork of a green track up the hillside. It climbs more steeply beneath a small plantation, then levels out to cross a stream. Go through a gateway and past a track leading down to old workings. *Between 1851-63 a mine here produced lead, copper and silver. In the 1880s it was worked for slate.* Keep ahead up the now walled track.

3 Just beyond its end, with the stone barn of 18thC Cyfanned Fawr (see **Walk 15**) ahead, turn RIGHT by a waymark post set in the wall. Follow the wall on your right and go through an old gateway. Keep ahead, soon bending RIGHT with the path down to a waymark post. Here, turn LEFT through an old gateway, then follow the waymarked

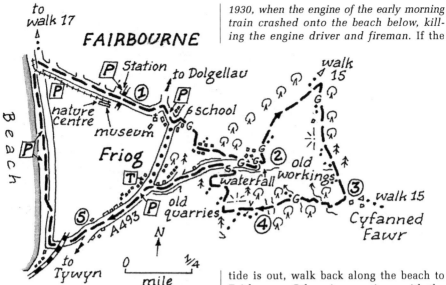

1930, when the engine of the early morning train crashed onto the beach below, killing the engine driver and fireman. If the

tide is out, walk back along the beach to Fairbourne. Otherwise, continue with the road, then go along the grass embankment by the sea defences, through the beach car park, and on along a pathway. At Penrhyn Stores, turn RIGHT along Beach Road back to the start.

path down near the stream. At a ruined stone barn, turn LEFT along its near side, and at its corner, go half-RIGHT for about 25 yards to reach a waymark post on a small ridge – *a prominent viewpoint*. Turn LEFT to drop down through the trees to go through a kissing gate and across a stream just before it tumbles down a narrow gorge. Continue ahead on the main path, soon descending in stages across the attractive tree-covered slope.

4 At a green track rising left, keep ahead to follow a faint path to a waymark post just above an old quarry about 50 yards ahead. Cross the stream and go across rough reedy ground to reach a wide track. Follow it as it meanders down the hillside past the quarry to the lane in the valley bottom. Turn LEFT and follow the lane to the A493. Cross the road and turn LEFT along the pavement through Friog.

5 By the old tollgate cottage, go along the minor road, soon passing through an arched railway bridge to reach the seafront. *Building the railway across the nearby steep cliffs was a major feat of engineering. Strangely, there were almost identical accidents on this section of line in 1883 and*

Fairbourne owns its existence to Arthur McDougal (of flour fame). In 1895, he purchased the Ynysfaig estate and adjacent land, with the intention to create an elite sea-side resort, to be called South Barmouth. His ambitious plans, which included a pier, were never fully realised by the time he sold the estate in 1912, being unable to compete with the better facilities of Barmouth. The village takes its name from the new railway station he had built in 1899 – a seemingly inappropriate English name in such a Welsh setting. Apparently, locals requested it be called 'Ynysfaig', but he refused on the grounds that the name boards had already been painted! The golf course and some original houses, at which he planted a rose bush, remain. Perhaps his greatest legacy was the horse drawn tramway, built originally for construction work, but extended to the ferry between 1897-98 and used to transport summer visitors. Without it the famous narrow gauge railway would never have developed.

35

CWM-LLWYD

DESCRIPTION An exhilarating 9½ mile walk on superb scenic high-level ancient trackways across open hills and upland valleys, with panoramic views, and featuring many early sites and monuments of archaelogical interest. The route rises north east from Llwyngwril to follow a prehistoric route across foothills, passing standing stones and an early settlement. It then rises again to follow Ffordd Ddu, reputedly an old Roman road, across steep slopes, reaching a height of 1315 feet, before descending through Cwm-llwyd. Another ancient trackway is then followed before a descent by lane takes you past Castel y Gaer hillfort. Allow about 5¼ hours.

START Llwyngwril [SH 592097]

DIRECTIONS Llwyngwril, with its own railway station, lies on the A493 coast road. On the northern side of the village centre, just off the A493 is a signposted car park.

Ffordd Ddu (Black Road) is an ancient mountain route running from Dolgellau to Llanegryn, from where other routes led into the valleys of the Dysynni and Dovey, and on through the Upper Severn valley to the English border. It had branches down to Arthog, Friog and Llwyngwril. It is believed to be part of the Roman Road network linking West Wales with garrisons at Chester and near Shrewsbury, a route serving smaller camps near the coast. During the Middle Ages it became an important route for local Welsh gentry seeking patronage with London and the Royal Court. It also attracted bandits, especially the notorious 'Red Men of Dinas Mawddwy'. It was used regularly as a coach road until the building of the Turnpike coastal road in the 19thC.

I Follow the A493 north through the village towards Friog. After about ⅓ mile, at a waymarked bridleway on the right by Llwyn Croft opposite a letter-box in the wall, turn RIGHT along a track to its end at Llwyn Du. *By the late 17thC many families in the area were Quakers, and nearby at Bryn*

Tallwyn is a Quaker burial ground dating from 1646. Keep ahead to go through a gate at the end of a long stone barn. Now bear RIGHT up alongside a wall, then after about 25 yards, swing sharp LEFT up to follow the bridleway alongside a wall on your left along the edge of a small wood – *associated with ancient Druid ceremonies.* Follow the bridleway up the hillside to reach open country via a small gate, and on up to join a lane. Turn LEFT along the lane. After going through a gate, when the lane bends right towards a house, keep straight ahead up a green track alongside a wall. The track soon bears LEFT up the exposed slopes parallel with the coast. *On the slopes above are ancient standing stones and a hut circle.* It then levels out – *with stunning new views across to Barmouth* – and heads inland, passing above a small ruin and on through two gates to join a lane.

2 Follow the gated lane across the wild upland landscape. *Just after passing sheepfolds, in the field on your left is a line of five prehistoric standing stones, two having fallen. Further down the field are hut circles.* Continue along the lane – *known locally as Ffordd Sarnau.* When you are joined by a fence on the left, on the slope below are the distinctive remains of a large Romano British hut circle settlement. The lane then descends, passing further standing stones, then goes through a plantation. At a waymarked path junction on the right, go half-RIGHT on a green track angling up through the plantation. Follow the track through the trees and on past a clearing – *site of a hut circle settlement* – to leave the plantation by a stile.

3 Now follow a clear path across high upland pasture, passing through a gate by a stream, and later rising steadily up to cross a stile by a wall corner. Keep ahead to

36

pass a commemorative plaque in the wall. *It records the Americans who were tragically killed on their way home.* Continue up to join a track. *This is Ffordd Ddu.* Turn RIGHT and follow this superb high-level gated track rising steadily across the steep slopes of Braich Ddu

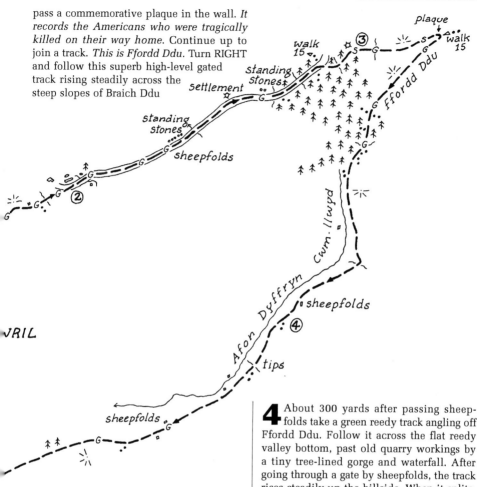

and on along the edge of a plantation, passing side tracks and a waymarked path. After going through a gate by a stream, the track soon passes two waymarked paths near the end of the plantation. It then begins a long gentle descent south through Cwm-llwyd, following the course of the Afon Dyffryn below, surrounded by bare hills. After crossing a stream, it then heads south-west along the wide river valley.

4 About 300 yards after passing sheepfolds take a green reedy track angling off Ffordd Ddu. Follow it across the flat reedy valley bottom, past old quarry workings by a tiny tree-lined gorge and waterfall. After going through a gate by sheepfolds, the track rises steadily up the hillside. When it splits, keep on up the RIGHT fork, through a gate and on with the track past a tiny plantation. At a crossroad of tracks keep ahead to walk by a line of telegraph poles – *with views of the Tarren Hills, Tywyn and the coast.* Cross a ladder-stile in a wall corner by a twin telegraph pole. Go ahead through two fields to reach a road. Turn RIGHT and at a junction, bear RIGHT along an attractive walled lane. After crossing a cattle-grid, the more open lane begins its descent to Llwyngwril, soon passing the remains of Castell y Gaer Iron Age hillfort, to reach the A493 by St. Celynnin's church. Turn RIGHT and follow the road back through the village to the start.

LLANGELYNIN & LLANEGRYN CHURCHES

DESCRIPTION A 5½ mile walk (**A**) using a network of field paths and old green tracks to explore the undulating countryside lying between the late 12thC church of St. Celynin in the coastal hamlet of Llangelynin, and the 13thC church at Llanegryn. Allow about 3½ hours. The route includes two shorter walks of 2¼ miles (**B**) and 4½ miles (**C**).

START Llangelynin [SH 572071]

DIRECTIONS The tiny hamlet of Llangelynin lies about 2 miles south-west of Llwyngwril, alongside the A493, where there is a large lay-by on the seaward side. It is also accessible by bus.

I Follow the lane down to visit the attractive stone church (information inside). Return to the A493. Cross the road and follow it LEFT with great care towards oncoming traffic for about ⅓ mile to turn RIGHT up a lane signposted to Prysgau-isaf. Follow it up the hillside. When it ends at a farmhouse, swing sharp RIGHT up a green track, through a gate, and follow it up the hillside – *enjoying good views to Barmouth , Shell Island, the Lleyn Peninsula and Bardsey Island*. Go through a gate and continue up the part-walled track. When you meet a stone wall directly ahead, at a junction of paths, turn RIGHT. (*For* **Walk B** *continue up the track, over a ladder-stile, on alongside the fence, and through a gap in the field corner. Head half-left up to go through an old gateway in the top corner. Follow the wall on your right, and on over a ladder-stile ahead. Pass to the left of a ruined barn, then turn right through a gate. Keep ahead to go through the left of two gateways, on across a field, and over a stile in the right hand corner. Follow the track right to point* **6**.)

2 For **Walk A**, immediately go half-LEFT to follow the old wall on your left up to cross a gate. Keep ahead along the field edge

and over another gate. Now go half-RIGHT up across the next field, over an old boundary and on through a gateway. Follow a path through the next field to an old boundary corner. Follow the boundary on your right, and at the field corner, bear LEFT along the field edge to go through a gate in the next corner. Go straight ahead to the boundary in front, and follow it LEFT. *In the distance is the Cadair Idris range.* Go through a gate in the corner, and on with the boundary to reach a lane by a ruin. *Here at Pant-gwyn is a crossroads of ancient trackways. The next section follows the course of an old green lane down to Blaidd.* Go half-RIGHT and through a gate on the left-hand side of outbuildings. Continue ahead – *with good views to Tywyn and, on a clear day, along the coast to Pembrokeshire* – through a gate, and on with an enclosed path, soon bending inland – *with views to the Tarren Hills.*

3 Just before the path descends, with gates on either side, you have a choice. (*For* **Walk C**, *turn right through the wooden gate, and keep ahead to follow another old green lane, past sheepfolds and through two gates to steadily descend the hillside to reach a waymarked path junction. Resume text at point* **5**.) For **Walk A** continue ahead down to cross a stile, and follow the green track, soon dropping down to go through a gate, and on to cross a ladder-stile just above Blaidd. Go down between outbuildings to cross a stile ahead. Go down the field edge, over two footbridges, and on over a ladder-stile in the field corner. Go across two fields, then along the next field edge above a stream to cross a footbridge by a small wood. Now go half-RIGHT, soon near the fence on your left, to go through a gate in the corner. Turn LEFT past a barn and farmhouse to the road by Llanegryn Church. Go ahead to pass in front of the war memorial and through the churchyard to visit the church. *This attractive 13thC church contains a splendid carved wooden rood loft and screen, reputed to come from Cymmer Abbey after the Dissolution of monasteries ordered by Henry VIII.*

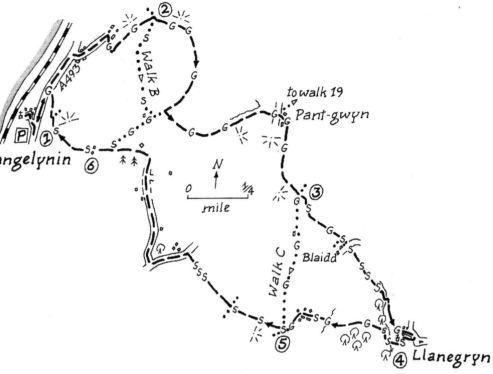

4 Retrace your steps, and just beyond the end of the church, turn RIGHT over a slate stile in the churchyard wall. Follow a path RIGHT alongside the wall and on down a field to cross a stile and footbridge over the stream. Go ahead through the trees, then bear RIGHT up a path to cross a ladder-stile into a field. Head half-RIGHT to go through a gate in the field/wood corner. Go along the wood edge, and at the wood/shrub corner head towards a telegraph pole by the far field boundary. Bear RIGHT alongside the boundary and on through a wooden gate in the fence ahead. Go up the small enclosure and over a ladder-stile in the left-hand corner below a farm. Go ahead, to follow a track up through the farm, bending LEFT beneath the house and follow the track through a gate to a waymarked path junction on the bend.

5 Here cross the stile by the footpath post. Walk ahead by the boundary up to cross a ladder-stile in the corner. Continue alongside the wall, over another ladder-stile and

footbridge, across a green track, and on up the slope ahead. Follow the waymarked path along the boundary to cross a stone stile in the wall corner. Bear RIGHT and follow the waymarked path over two further stone stiles, then keep ahead with the boundary on your right to reach a lane. Follow it LEFT to a junction. Here, turn RIGHT and follow the lane up to its end by a stone barn and on along a track. When it splits, keep ahead, and follow the track round to pass between a plantation and a large building, and on to reach a house.

6 Follow the path through Ty Newydd to cross a slate stile above the house. Continue ahead across the field and over an old wall by a waymark post. Now bear half-RIGHT down the steep slope towards the great expanse sea, over a stile and on down the slope. The path zig zags before angling down to go through a kissing gate onto the A493. Cross the road and follow it LEFT back to the start.

PRONUNCIATION

These basic points should help non-Welsh speakers

Welsh	English equivalent
c	always hard, as in **c**at
ch	as in the Scottish word lo**ch**
dd	as th in **th**en
f	as **f** in o**f**
ff	as **ff** in o**ff**
g	always hard as in **g**ot
ll	no real equivalent. It is like 'th' in **th**en, but with an 'L' sound added to it, giving '**thlan**' for the pronunciation of the Welsh 'Llan'.

In Welsh the accent usually falls on the last-but-one syllable of a word.

KEY TO THE MAPS

- ➔ Walk route and direction
- ═══ Metalled road
- ─ ─ ─ Unsurfaced road
- •••• Footpath/route adjoining walk route
- ～～ River/stream
- ♣ ♤ Trees
- ▄▄▄ Railway
- **G** Gate
- **S** Stile
- **F.B.** Footbridge
- ☼ Viewpoint
- P Parking
- T Telephone
- Caravan site

THE COUNTRY CODE

Be safe – plan ahead and follow relevant signs

Leave gates and property as you find them

Protect plants and animals, and take your litter home

Keep dogs under close control

Be considerate to other people

I would like to thank staff at Gwynedd Council Highways Department, the Archives in Dolgellau, the Snowdonia National Park Area Office, and Gwynedd Archaeological Trust for their invaluable advice and assistance. Also, special thanks to Dora and Glanmor Roberts at Garthyfog, Arthog, for their hospitality and friendship over many years.

Published by
Kittiwake
3 Glantwymyn Village Workshops,
Glantwymyn, Machynlleth, Montgomeryshire
SY20 8LY

© Text & map research: David Berry 2002
© Maps: Kittiwake 2002

Reprints 2007, 2008, 2009.

Cover photographs by David Berry – large: Looking across the mouth of the Mawddach (Walk **2**); inset: Standing stone (Walk **19**).

Care has been taken to be accurate. However neither the author nor the publisher can accept responsibility for any errors which may appear, or their consequences. If you are in doubt about any access, check before you proceed.

Printed by MWL, Pontypool.
ISBN: 978 1 902302 21 8